UPPER ELEMENTARY
READING LESSONS

UPPER ELEMENTARY READING LESSONS

Case Studies of Real Teaching

Marilyn J. Chambliss
and
Linda Valli

ROWMAN & LITTLEFIELD PUBLISHERS, INC.

Lanham • Boulder • New York • Toronto • Plymouth, UK

Published by Rowman & Littlefield Publishers, Inc.
A wholly owned subsidary of The Rowman & Littlefield Publishing Group, Inc.
4501 Forbes Boulevard, Suite 200, Lanham, Maryland 20706
http://www.rowmanlittlefield.com

Estover Road, Plymouth PL6 7PY, United Kingdom

British Library Cataloguing in Publication Information Available

Library of Congress Cataloging-in-Publication Data

Chambliss, Marilyn J.
  Upper elementary reading lessons : case studies of real teaching / Marilyn Chambliss,
Linda Valli.
      p. cm.
  Includes bibliographical references.
  ISBN 978-1-4422-1193-3 (pbk. : alk. paper) — ISBN 978-1-4422-1194-0
(electronic)
  1. Reading (Elementary)—United States—Case studies. 2. Action research in
education—United States—Case studies. 3. Language arts (Elementary)—Case
studies. 4. English language—Study and teaching (Elementary)—Case studies. 5.
Critical pedagogy—Case studies. I. Valli, Linda, 1947- II. Title.
  LB1576.C4183 2010
  372.4—dc22

                                                                    2011004558

∞™ The paper used in this publication meets the minimum requirements of American National Standard for Information Sciences—Permanence of Paper for Printed
Library Materials, ANSI/NISO Z39.48-1992.

Printed in the United States of America

Contents

Part II: Perspectives on Teaching: Commentaries

Preface

Teachers benefit from concrete examples that illustrate good practice. With that in mind, we have crafted eight reading cases, with accompanying commentaries, which depict real lessons in real classrooms. These are lessons delivered without rehearsal or extraordinary crafting. Thus while each case highlights at least one particular dimension of good teaching, each case also will likely evoke some dilemmas and inspire ideas for improving that lesson and one's own lessons. While individual teachers can read and learn from these cases on their own, they likely are more powerfully used in group settings.

The cases present multiple goals of reading instruction (vocabulary development, reading comprehension, linking reading and writing) across genres (narrative, exposition or informational text, and poetry) and exemplify an array of underlying principles of good practice. They also illustrate many of the newly adopted Common Core State Standards in English language arts and literacy in history/social studies, science, and technical subjects. An important feature of these standards is the notion of text complexity, as discussed in appendix A (www. corestandards.org/assets/Appendix_A.pdf). The specific goals of literacy instruction for a particular standard often remain identical across several grades; what differs is text complexity from simple texts in the earlier grades to more complex texts in later grades. A special sidebar feature in our casebook links each case with one or more corresponding standards.

Appreciation is owed to more individuals and organizations than we can name. First, we thank our funder: the Interagency Education Research Initiative (IERI # 0115389), which was a combined effort of the National Science Foundation, the U.S. Department of Education, and the National Institutes of Health. Next, we thank our co-researchers on this project, Robert Croninger, Patricia Alexander, and Jeremy Price, who pushed and improved our thinking at every turn, and all of the graduate assistants and post-docs who contributed to the case collection, coding, and writing, especially Heather Ruetschlin Schugar and Judith Concha. We also thank Patti Belcher, acquisitions editor at Rowman & Littlefield, for seeing the pedagogical value of these cases and for her helpful and speedy response to all our questions. Last, because pseudonyms are used throughout this volume, special appreciation goes to the "real" teachers behind these cases, who graciously let us into their classrooms so that we could share with you these case studies of real teaching.

While individual teachers can read and learn from these cases on their own, they are more powerfully used in preservice teacher preparation programs, in-service professional development sessions, and school-based inquiry groups. For teacher educators, course instructors, and staff developers, a Facilitator's Guide has been written to accompany the text. Please contact Rowman & Littlefield at textbooks@rowman.com on how to access this guide. Features of the Facilitator's Guide include:

- **An expanded research base.** Seminal chapters and research articles only referenced in the Guide that facilitators can use to lead discussion and ground the cases even more firmly in theory, research, and practice.
- **Instructional approaches for each chapter.** Key aspects highlighted with analytic comments to guide discussion.
- **Experienced instructor insight.** Four new commentaries written by Heather Ruetschlin Schugar, a reading methods instructor, describing her approaches and insights in using the cases.
- **Applications of case studies.** Suggestions on using the cases with preservice and in-service teachers.

Alternative Thematic Frameworks

READING INSTRUCTION PRINCIPLES

Choose Genres to Teach Strategies

Use Established Programs to Teach Strategies

Link Reading and Writing

Read to prepare to write — Case 5
Word study to improve spelling and decoding — Case 1

LEARNER-CENTERED PSYCHOLOGICAL PRINCIPLES

Knowledge principle	Cases 1, 3, 4, 5, 6, 7
Strategic processing principle	Cases 1, 2, 3, 4, 6, 7
Developmental principle	Cases 3, 7
Motivational principle	Cases 1, 2, 3, 5, 6, 7
Social context principle	Cases 2, 3, 4, 5, 6, 7

TOPIC/GENRE CONTENTS

Narrative	Cases 3, 4, 5, 6, 7
Poetry	Cases 2, 6
Exposition	Cases 6, 8
Vocabulary	Cases 1, 3, 6, 7
Decoding/spelling	Case 1
Fluency	Case 2
Comprehension strategies	Cases 4, 5, 6, 7, 8

INSTRUCTIONAL LEVEL CONTEXTS

English as a Second Language (ESL) students	Cases 1, 3
Special education and ESL students	Cases 2, 3
Heterogeneous/grade-level groups	Cases 5, 7, 8
Advanced group	Case 5

COMMON CORE STANDARDS

---

1 Although the Common Core State Standards list this under Grade 3, the expository text used in this case is at a higher grade level. Good classroom teachers at these higher grade levels would build on students' third-grade knowledge of using text features to locate information in more difficult texts they had not previously read.

Introduction

Marilyn Chambliss and Linda Valli

E very teacher understands that knowing what to do in a concrete situation is not the same as knowing how to do it. Engaging students in worthwhile learning requires more than a knowledge of underlying principles of good teaching. It demands considerable practice as well as concrete images of what that teaching might look like in specific situations. To teach in ways that are different from ways we've been taught (through textbooks, worksheets, recitations), we need alternative images. Changing habits of practice, and expanding our notions of what is possible, requires the ability to imagine something different.

The purpose of this book is to create some of those images: descriptive cases of illustrative reading lessons that represent a range of teaching practices. Cases provide a rich source of material for deeper understandings of the complex, ill-structured practice of teaching. Their narrative structure is well suited to capturing teachers' knowledge in practice. Unlike traditional textbooks, "the verisimilitude of cases helps make related theories useful and relevant, decreases the danger of participants developing inert knowledge, and increases the probability that knowledge will transfer to similar situations in the future" (Levin 1999, 148). Judy Shulman (1992) calls cases "a piece of controllable reality" that are positioned between the prescriptive world of textbooks and the messy world of real classrooms. This makes them a particularly useful pedagogical tool. Reading, reflecting on, and discussing how another teacher approached a particular topic, strategy, or concept opens up new vistas for learning.

The pedagogical cases in this book were written from authentic, unrehearsed lessons taught by regular classroom teachers to diverse groups of real students. As a collection, the cases embody the notion that teaching is multi-dimensional, that it has different characteristics across and within subject matter (Chambliss and Graeber 2003; Valli et al. 2004).[1] While each case illustrates a particular dimension of good teaching, several cases have features in common. The Alternative Thematic Frameworks chart follows the table of contents and regroups the cases according to common topics; the Common Core State Standards (2010); whether the lesson was primarily geared to students who were below, at, or above grade level; and whether students were English language learners or students in special education. Three of the cases are accompanied by the thoughtful reflections of an array of commentators: a classroom teacher, a teacher educator, and a speaker of other languages scholar. In addition, part II of the casebook,

---

1 See the companion volume, Graeber, Valli, and Newton *Upper Elementary Mathematics Lessons: Case Studies of Real Teaching* (Lanham, MD: Rowman & Littlefield, 2011).

"Perspectives on Teaching," presents more general commentaries that analyze good teaching across cases.

We encourage readers to use the Alternative Thematic Frameworks to guide their case selections, to depart from the customary way of reading a book (i.e., from first chapter to last), and, instead, to purposefully select cases that are most relevant to their situations. As you read a case, think about how it can inform and help improve your teaching. Reading the commentaries after that reflection will provide additional opportunities for growth. Because this casebook will often be used with groups, we have included a Facilitator's Guide to assist the instructor, staff developer, or group leader.[2]

HOW THESE CASES WERE SELECTED AND WRITTEN

These eight reading cases are drawn from a four-year study of fourth and fifth grade mathematics and reading instruction.[3] We selected these grades and subjects because mathematics and reading are arguably the two most important subjects in the elementary school curriculum, yet many fourth and fifth graders still struggle with foundational literacy and numeracy skills. Because some groups of children are particularly vulnerable with regard to literacy and numeracy, we selected schools that were culturally diverse

---

2 Contact Rowman & Littlefield at textbooks@rowman.com for information on how to access the guide.

3 The work reported herein was supported by the Interagency Education Research Initiative (IERI # 0115389), a combined effort of the National Science Foundation, the U.S. Department of Education, and the National Institutes of Health. The opinions expressed in this manuscript are our own and do not reflect the positions and policy of the National Science Foundation, the U.S. Department of Education, or the National Institutes of Health.

and had relatively high rates of students from poor and low-income families (30 to 90 percent).

Multiple factors were considered in selecting case study teachers, including student achievement, observation data, and nominations. We began by examining student achievement data for our pool of approximately seventy teachers each year, noting, in particular, teachers whose students achieved higher than predicted scores on standardized tests given by the state and school district. We then analyzed data from classroom observers, ranked teachers on their overall high-quality ratings, and made a list of teachers to consider. Members of the research team also asked for written recommendations from observers and met to discuss teachers who were high on one or more criteria (student achievement, observer rating, observer nomination). By the end of that meeting, the team had selected the final group of case study teachers. In addition to selecting teachers who exhibited various characteristics of good teaching in the lessons we observed, we wanted to include a range of contexts: both fourth and fifth grade classrooms, classes ranging from special education to gifted and talented, classrooms with a high percent of English language learners, lessons that focused on different topics and genres, and so forth.

Observers from the team audio-taped and took narrative field notes of each lesson. They interviewed the teachers after each observation, asking teachers to reflect on the lesson, their students, the curriculum, and the school climate. The research team also collected classroom materials, worksheets, and handouts from the case study lessons. Subsequently, members of the team transcribed the tapes and inserted the field notes into the transcripts for analysis. Our reading expert, Marilyn Chambliss, made the final decision on which lessons were case worthy. A writing team then met regularly to develop procedures for coding cases, to establish a standard protocol for case writing, and to decide on the dimensions of quality to be exemplified in each case.

Because we believe that teaching should be closely guided by understandings of how people learn (Bransford, Brown, and Cocking 1999), we drew on five research domains that were core to the development of the American Psychological Association's (APA) learner-centered psychological principles. Those domains, used for case selection and development, indicate, for example, that good teachers promote deep, principled learning of content; encourage the development of cognitive and metacognitive skills; motivate students to engage deeply in subject matter; address individual and developmental differences among students; and create inclusive, affirming, and successful learning environments (Alexander & Murphy 1998). These principles are explicitly brought out in the cases, and the Thematic Organization chart groups cases according to the five principles.

But differences in subject areas, curricular topics, students, and curricular materials make different demands on teachers' content and pedagogical expertise, signaling the importance of drawing on domain-specific research. While this research is consistent with learner-centered psychological principles, the particular manifestations of exemplary teaching differ by subject matter. The reading cases developed for this text exemplify instruction recommended by the learned societies (IRA and NCTE 1996) as well as empirical research (Kamil et al. 2000; National Reading Panel 2000; Taylor and Pearson 2002). This exemplary teaching includes (a) the study of the systems and structures of language (e.g., spelling and vocabulary patterns; genre characteristics), (b) practice with a wide range of strategies to interpret and create interesting and challenging texts of a variety of genres (e.g., visualization of the make-believe world in science fiction), (c) help with making personal responses to texts (e.g., the choice of a favorite character), and (d) links between reading and writing (e.g., analysis of an autobiography to prepare to write an autobiography).

For reading, studying the systems and structures of language promotes deep, principled learning of content. Practicing with a wide range of strategies to interpret and create texts of a variety of genres encourages the development of cognitive and metacognitive skills. Helping students respond to texts personally motivates students to engage deeply in subject matter. Tailoring instruction to their interests and needs addresses individual and developmental differences among students. Classrooms where students and teachers treat one another with respect as they work together to complete their tasks create an inclusive, affirming, and successful learning environment. These learning principles cut across the eight cases of reading instruction.

As mentioned earlier, case commentators were selected who could provide insights on good teaching from different perspectives: special education, second-language acquisition, moral dimensions, cognitive psychology, and subject matter expertise. Wanting both research and practitioner perspectives, we also invited an award-winning principal and an expert elementary school teacher to comment on the lessons. These commentaries bring out the underlying principles and multiple aspects of good teaching. We urge readers to read and reflect on the cases before turning to the commentaries. This will foster both independent thinking and deeper reflection.

WHAT TYPE OF CASES?

The case literature can be divided into two basic categories—or ends of a spectrum: dilemma cases and exemplary cases (Barnett-Clarke 2001). Dilemma cases are structured around problems of practice, such as cross-cultural communications or subject matter misunderstandings, and ask readers to ponder what they would do in that situation (Carter 1999; Merseth 1996; L. Shulman 1992). Exemplary cases, on the other hand, are designed to portray good practice—to depict a teaching method, classroom organization, or way of interacting with students. Through their concrete detail, they illustrate principles of good teaching and ground theoretical understandings (Merseth 1996; Shulman 2004). In this type of case, "teaching skills or instructional approaches (e.g., cooperative learning or inquiry teaching) are made concrete by portraying a teacher using the method in an actual classroom" (Carter 1999, 167). While both types of cases can serve multiple purposes (e.g., illustrate theory, promote reflection, develop problem-solving skills), each is better suited to accomplishing some goals more than others.

We have elected to prepare a book of cases that primarily illustrate, or "exemplify," particular aspects of teaching, but also evoke teaching dilemmas. The cases are not "exemplary" in all aspects. Indeed, in our observations of hundreds of lessons we rarely, if ever, saw a lesson that we would deem "perfect." But we did often see lessons in which some aspect of sound teaching was highly visible. It is these features of good teaching that the cases highlight. In this sense the cases reflect aspects of exemplary cases. And, knowing how hard good teaching can be, we wanted to present some "images of the possible." As Lee Shulman (1992) writes, "Case studies of . . . well-grounded exemplars of good practice . . . portray concrete human images of activities and values worthy of emulation. They thus serve to stimulate . . . alternative forms of practice that are rooted in real teaching" (8–9). This does not mean that every teacher action in every case is perfect. It does mean that the teaching in these cases is more accomplished, and more difficult, than immediately meets the eye.

But helping teachers consider what might be improved in a lesson is probably even more valuable than providing exemplars. As Barnett-Clarke (2001) cautions, pure exemplars can oversimplify teaching and call attention to mere surface characteristics, whereas dilemma-focused cases can "pull participants into an inquiry mode" (311). The Facilitator's Guide includes questions that will help stimulate readers to consider how a lesson might be improved, whether the teacher might have considered a different approach, or why the approach was "good" for the situation described. Believing that "a good teacher is not one who can master the teaching model but rather can master diverse situations, that is, come to terms with a wide range of events and contingencies" (Carter 1999, 175), we ask readers to consider the cases in light of what is known about the context and to ponder some "what ifs" for the cases.

WHY THESE SUBJECT-MATTER CASES?

We have also elected to focus these cases on the teaching of subject matter. Over the past decade or so, education researchers have become increasingly aware of the importance of teachers' knowledge of subject matter for student learning. This has been accompanied by greater understanding of the differences in pedagogical expertise across subject areas and the complexity of learning to teach different subjects (Grossman et al. 2005; Stevens et al. 2005). We propose that elementary school teachers, who typically teach several subject matters, can find the differences in pedagogical knowledge in mathematics and reading to be particularly challenging. Because cases enhance teachers' professional knowledge (Lundeberg and Scheurman 1997) and improve their ability to make well-reasoned decisions (Grossman 2005), using cases about the teaching of specific subject matter should be a high priority with both preservice and in-service teachers (Shulman 2004). Wilson's (1992) claim that the subject-matter knowledge needed for good teaching requires new methods still holds.

Since these cases were written, most states across the country have adopted the Common Core Standards for English language arts and literacy in history/social studies, science, and technical subjects (www.corestandards .org/). Developed under the leadership of the Council of Chief State School Officers (CCSSO) and the National

Governors Association (NGA), these standards are the first widely adopted national attempt to specify the literacy skills that students would need to be college and career ready. Each of the cases in this volume addresses one or more of these standards, which are identified in the Alternative Thematic Frameworks and on the first page of each case, discussed in the preface, and briefly explained in the Case Setting and Overview for several of the cases.

PREVIEW OF TEACHERS AND STUDENTS

The five teachers portrayed in these cases range in experience from one to more than thirty years. Three are female and two are male. All are European American with the exception of Ms. Peterson, who has a Caribbean heritage. Each of these teachers had a culturally diverse classroom of students, which we describe in the case overviews by using the school district's official categories: African American, Asian, Hispanic, and White. Although somewhat limiting and awkward,[4] these categories provide us with the most comprehensive and systematic data available.

We also use three acronyms, taken from official records, to describe the student population: FARMs, ESOL, and IEP:

- FARMs stands for Free and Reduced Meals and is an indicator of poverty.

---

4 For example, some students classified as African American had been born and raised in countries of Africa, whereas many students classified as Asian had been born and raised in the United States. We have no information regarding the classification of the growing numbers of Arab Americans and recent immigrants from the Middle East.

- ESOL stands for English for Speakers of Other Languages and is used to identify English language learners who were assigned to these supplementary classes based on their levels of English language proficiency.
- IEP stands for Individualized Education Plan and denotes special education students.

Because students sometimes move in and out of these categories, and because their school history is relevant, we use the school district phrase "were currently or had been" in our case overviews.

PREVIEW OF CASES

To prepare the reader for the case narrative, we begin each case by describing the setting and giving a general overview. Knowing something about the teacher, students, time of year, classroom, and case content gives a sense of "being there" and helps us better understand teachers' actions. We encourage readers to picture themselves in the classroom, watching the lessons unfold. As you read, think about the teachers' pedagogical moves, what they were trying to accomplish, and what you might have done in that situation. Raise questions and reflect on the questions at the end of the case. Use the titles, which highlight specific aspects of good teaching, to guide your selections. Remember that these are not raw transcripts of lessons you are reading, but cases carefully crafted to serve as teaching tools. Here is a snapshot of the eight reading cases. Note that we have ordered them according to the order in which the research in the Report of the National Reading Panel

(2000) is presented: alphabetics, fluency, vocabulary, and text comprehension.

To encourage even the newest teachers, we start with two cases of Ms. Hinton, a first-year teacher. In the first case, we see Ms. Hinton as she meets with her spelling groups. Far from having students simply memorize the spelling of a word, Ms. Hinton builds on their understanding of word meanings and spelling rules, engaging them in conversations about etymology and word study to link reading and writing and support their developing literacy. The second case took place during that same class and shows Ms. Hinton engaged in whole class instruction, teaching and modeling fluency in the reading of poetry to prepare students to perform the reading of a poem of their choice during a subsequent class. We follow up Ms. Hinton's fluency case with Case 3, in which Ms. Gabriel, the most experienced teacher, presents two types of vocabulary instruction. Developing her instruction from words students identified as problematic in the novels they were reading, Ms. Gabriel has them prepare for the lesson by using a concept of definition map and models how to use context and background knowledge to determine word meanings, allowing readers to compare different approaches for teaching vocabulary.

The next four cases focus on teaching comprehension strategies. In Case 4, we visit Mr. DiLoretto's classroom, where he is teaching a comprehension lesson that immediately followed a mathematics lesson on geometry.[5] Taking advantage of that day's discussion of "attributes" in the mathematics lesson, he focuses student attention on

---

5 See Case 7 in the companion *Upper Elementary Math Lessons.*

"character traits," and how they are similar to attributes, first modeling for the whole group the type of discussions they should have in their small groups. In Case 5, we return to Ms. Gabriel's classroom where she meets with a second reading group to discuss the autobiography they are reading. Because her main purpose for this text is to prepare students to write their own autobiographies, she spends considerable time having them make personal connections to the text. The sixth case we encounter is of Mr. Dunbar, who undertakes the challenging task of teaching metacognitive skills to students across three genres (narrative, exposition, and poetry) in one class period. In Case 7, the third group of students in Ms. Gabriel's class is reading science fiction. Knowing that her students find this genre difficult, Ms. Gabriel employs numerous strategies, most notably connections, visualization, and prediction, to help them comprehend text.

In Case 8, Ms. Peterson engages her students with expository, rather than narrative text, working with them in small groups to develop previewing strategies. In this last case, Ms. Peterson bridges reading instruction with social studies instruction, another important subject matter that elementary teachers are responsible for teaching.

I
THE TEACHING
OF READING:
LESSON CASES

Case 1
Word Study that
Supports Reading
and Writing

Fourth-Grade Reading Lesson

CASE SETTING

Emma Hinton, a first-year teacher at Brookfield Elementary School, taught this word study lesson in a
portable building near the end of the school year, June 2,
from 9:30–11:00. Ms. Hinton's class was a heterogeneous
mix of twenty-four students. Their reading levels varied
from second to eighth grade. Ms. Hinton had two ESOL
students in her class. However, many of her students' first
language was Spanish. During this lesson, Ms. Hinton met
with two small groups of students. The students in the
second small group were native Spanish speakers.

CASE OVERVIEW

The following case illustrates how a word study lesson supports reading and writing through the development of students' decoding skills and word meanings. During this lesson, Ms. Hinton supported her students by facilitating discussions on and asking probing questions about (Wilkinson and Silliman 2000) the pronunciation, spelling, and meaning of words (Bear and Templeton 1998; Templeton and Morris 2000). This lesson included a focus on using letter-sound correspondences and morphology (e.g., roots and affixes) to read accurately unfamiliar words out of context, a Common Core Standard. Ms. Hinton had an easy rapport with her students.

RELATED COMMON CORE STATE STANDARD

Grades 3–5
Reading Foundational Skills
Standard 3:

- Know and apply grade-level phonics and word analysis skills in decoding words.
- Use combined knowledge of all letter-sound correspondences, syllabication patterns, and morphology (e.g., roots and affixes) to read accurately unfamiliar multisyllabic words in context and out of context.

THE CASE

Distinguishing among Words with Similar Letters/Sounds

Ms. Hinton began this word study lesson by calling a small group of students to a table in the back of the classroom. Sitting so she could see the entire class, she handed out a packet of papers to this group of students that included a week's worth of activities and worksheets for the students to complete.

A list of words was displayed at the top of the first sheet of paper. Ms. Hinton had the students look at the words *quite*, *quiet*, and *quit* and asked them why she might put them on a spelling test. She directed her question to the group, but asked a student named Elena to tell her why. Elena stated, "They are all *quiet*." Ms. Hinton responded, "Are they all *quiet*?" "Yeah," Elena said. Ms. Hinton responded by reading each word out loud: "*Quiet. Quite. Quit.*" Ms. Hinton continued, "Everyone, put your finger on *quiet*. *Qw-i-et*. Very good." Elena offered another response, "Because all three of them have *q*s." Ms. Hinton began to redirect, "How many syllables in *quiet*?" Several students responded, "Two." She asked the students to put their hand under their chin and say *quiet*. Then she asked how many times their hands hit their chins when they said *quiet*. The students responded, "Two."

Ms. Hinton moved on to the next word, *quite*. "Do we say the *e* at the end of that word?" she asked. Several students responded, "No." Ms. Hinton continued, "Why not? Why don't I say *quite-e*? What do we call that *e* at the end?" Andy responded, "It's a vowel." "It's a vowel," Ms. Hinton repeated. Then Andy offered another response, "It's a silent *e*." Ms. Hinton said, "Silent *e*. That silent *e* is very powerful. What does it do to the *i* in *quite*?" Andy continued, "It takes the *i* sound and makes it long."

The group continued, looking at the third word, *quit*. Ms. Hinton asked similar questions, prompting her students to access their prior knowledge of decoding. The students quickly came to the understanding that the word is pronounced *quit* and not *quite* because it didn't have the silent *e* at the end. Ms. Hinton stated that *quiet*, *quite*, and *quit* could be mixed up easily.

The group continued looking at the words on the list to make connections to other words. The words *whose* and *who's* led the students to discuss apostrophes. This discussion helped them recall that apostrophes are used to show possession and contractions. The students determined that *who's* was a contraction meaning *who is*. Then Ms. Hinton asked about the meaning of *whose*. Petra answered, "Who it belongs to." Ms. Hinton responded, "We said we used an apostrophe to show who it belongs to, didn't we? But here we have a whole different word when we're doing who it belongs to. Why do you think they did that? Why don't we just use an apostrophe? Could we ever tell the difference? Would it be hard to tell the difference between 'who is' and 'who it belongs to'? It would be difficult. I mean, there are many contractions. That would be difficult. That's why we have a separate word. So w-h-o-s-e means?" Elena responded, "Who it belongs to." Ms. Hinton affirmed her answer.

The group continued looking at their words on the list. They looked at *were*, *we're*, and *where*. Ms. Hinton pointed to the word *were* and said, "Put your finger on it. What is that word? Who can tell me what that word is? Andy? Third row, third column." Andy responded, "*Where*." Ms. Hinton said, "Spell it." Andy responded, "*W-e-r-e*." Ms. Hinton replied, "*Were. Were. Were*. Everyone look at it. Say it. *Were*." Everyone repeated the word *were*. Ms. Hinton continued, "What does that mean? Use it in a sentence. Who can use that in a sentence? Jimmy?" Jimmy said, "They were sitting in the chair." The students discussed the word *were* with Ms. Hinton. She pointed out that it is the past tense of the verb "to be."

Then the group discussed the word *we're*. "What kind of word is that?" Ms. Hinton asked. Marianna responded, "Um, two or more people." Ms. Hinton said, "Look at the word. *We're*." Another student responded, "It's a contraction." Ms. Hinton continued, "*We're*. What does that mean? What kind of word is that? Can you use it in a sentence?" Marianna replied, "We're going to the mall." Ms. Hinton responded, "We're going to the mall. We are going to the mall. So, what kind of a word is that?" Marianna said, "A contraction."

Using Knowledge of English to Pronounce Words

Ms. Hinton called a second small group of students to the back table. This group also had a packet of activities and worksheets, which each student brought to the table. In this packet was a list of words. The words were displayed in a column on the left side of the paper. Parallel to each word was a sentence that contained the word to provide context. Beneath each word, displayed in bold letters, was a phonetic representation. Ms. Hinton pronounced each word and had the group repeat each word after her.

After her students repeated the word *eliminate*, Ms. Hinton initiated a discussion. She said, "Now, the beginning of that word, what is the letter?" Some students said, "A" and some said, "E." Ms. Hinton confirmed that it began with the letter "E" and asked, "How do we pronounce a short *e*? Eh, eh. But, how do we pronounce this word? Ih-liminate. What's going on here?" Another student stated, "It's kind of English." Ms. Hinton concurred, "It is kind of English, isn't it? If we were speaking Spanish, the vowels would be the same all the time, right? ah, eh, ee, oh, oo." Ms. Hinton continued, "So be careful, especially those . . ." Another child responded, "Who are Spanish?" "Who Spanish is their main language or their second language," said Ms. Hinton. "Eh, ih, eliminate. Okay. Got that?"

Using Background Knowledge to Determine Word Meaning

The group continued going over words in their list. Ms. Hinton said each word and her students repeated them. After Ms. Hinton pronounced the word *forsake*, the students repeated the word after her. Then she asked, "What does *forsake* mean? Don't read me the definition. Who's heard that before? Forsake. Brandon?" Brandon said he didn't know what it meant. Ms. Hinton pressed on, "Where have you heard it before?" Brandon responded that he heard it on TV. Ms. Hinton asked if he knew where and Brandon said, "Um, on the Disney Channel." Ms. Hinton asked, "And what was it in reference to? What was it about?" Brandon said he didn't know. Ms. Hinton asked the rest of the group, "What is Brandon trying to do right now?" A student responded, "Trying to think back." Ms. Hinton said, "Make a connection, okay, and that's a good thing." She asked another student, Carlton, if he had heard it before. Carlton said, "I read it in a book." "In a book?" Ms. Hinton said. "And what was it talking about in the book?" Carlton said he couldn't remember, "but I think it was like a God-forsaken walk." Ms. Hinton responded, "A God-forsaken walk. You hear it in a lot of religious things, okay." Then Brandon responded, "And *Lord of the Rings*, they have it, a God-forsaken world." "Yeah, right," Ms. Hinton responded, "Well, let's look at the definition. To have nothing more to do with; to turn one's back on. Ooh." Another student linked the definition to the idea that if one became really rich and dumped all of his friends, he would be forsaking his friends. In response, Ms. Hinton said, "You dump all your friends when you're rich, huh? Have you ever heard that phrase, 'You better be nice to all the people on the way up because you're going to see them again on the way down'? Okay, when you're going up in popularity, do you always stay that popular or that rich?" The students responded, "No." Then, Ms. Hinton connected the word *forsake* to their last novel dealing with the rules of chivalry. She asked, "What do you think a rule would be, using the word *forsake*?" A student stated, "Never forsake your . . ." Ms. Hinton continued, "Never forsake your friends because?" Another student said, "Because when you go up . . .." "You may need them some day, right?" Ms. Hinton finished.

Using Affixes and Roots to Determine Word Meaning

Later in the same lesson, Ms. Hinton began a discussion that led the students to analyze words according to their affixes and root word patterns. The discussion began with the students determining the meaning of the word *trio*. Ms. Hinton stated, "Trio. What do you see in trio?" Carlton responded, "A *t*, an *r*, an *i*, and an *o*." Several other students responded, "*Tri*." Then Ms. Hinton asked, "Which means?" Several students responded, "Three." Ms. Hinton stated, "Three. Thank you. What part of speech? What did we call that?" Several students responded, "Prefix." Ms. Hinton asked, "Can it stand by itself?" The students were confused by this question. Some answered, "Yes" and some answered, "No." Ms. Hinton repeated the question. A student responded, "It's a root." Ms. Hinton continued, "Root. Can it stand by itself? No. Do we say *tri*—not *t-r-e-e*, but *t-r-i*, is that by itself?" Several students responded, "No." At this point, Ms. Hinton asked, "Is it like from Greek and Latin?" Several students responded, "Yeah." Ms. Hinton continued, "Yeah. So that was a root. What was the base? The base part of the word?" A student stated, "It could be itself in English." Ms. Hinton confirmed, "It could be by itself in English, right?" Brandon stated, "Like tricycle." Ms. Hinton repeated, "Tricycle. The tri means?" Several students responded, "Three." Ms. Hinton asked, "So what do you think a *trio* is?" Carlton said, "Three people. A group of three. A group of three people."

QUESTIONS

1. Why didn't Ms. Hinton just tell the students the difference between *who's* and *whose*? What did she do instead?
2. What teaching strategies did Ms. Hinton use to increase her students' knowledge of word meanings? How are Ms. Hinton's teaching decisions indicative of high-quality teaching?
3. How did Ms. Hinton develop her students' decoding skills and word meanings?

Case 2
Performing Poetry:
Explicit Modeling of Fluency

Fourth-Grade Reading Lesson

CASE SETTING

This fourth grade reading lesson was taught by Emma Hinton at Brookfield Elementary School on June 2. The lesson took place at the beginning of the school day in the portable classroom located outside of the main school building. The class consisted of a diverse population of students, including several second language learners as well as those identified as special education students. This reading class was heterogeneous in that there were varying levels of reading ability. Some students were reading below grade level while others were reading on or above grade level. This particular lesson involved the whole group of students and focused on reading fluency. Specifically, the lesson demonstrated to students various techniques for "performing" a poem for an audience.

CASE OVERVIEW

The following excerpts were taken from a fourth grade reading class in which Ms. Hinton explicitly modeled reading fluency (Worthy and Broaddus 2002), characterized by word accuracy, automaticity, and prosody (Hudson, Lane, and Pullen 2005). Although Ms. Hinton did not directly refer to fluency, her instruction focused on various techniques for reading a poem aloud or what she referred to as "performing" a poem. Students had studied poetry earlier in the school year, so the teacher activated their prior knowledge of poetic devices (Anderson and Pearson 1984). Ms. Hinton engaged her students and created an inclusive lesson that involved all students, regardless of reading ability. Ms. Hinton chose to focus on fluency because it provided all of her students, including her struggling readers, the opportunity to practice and perform a poem. The lesson addresses how to read poetry orally with accuracy, appropriate rate, and expression, one of the Common Core Standards for grades 3 to 5.

RELATED COMMON CORE STATE STANDARD

Grades 3–5
Reading Foundational Skills
Standard 4:

- Read with sufficient accuracy and fluency to support comprehension.
- Read grade-level prose and poetry orally with accuracy, appropriate rate, and expression.

THE CASE

Ms. Hinton began the lesson by activating students' prior knowledge about poetry. She asked students if they could name language patterns seen in poetry. Students named various examples, such as onomatopoeia, alliteration, and figurative language like similes and metaphors. Once students named a language pattern, the teacher probed further to elicit meaning and examples. When Ms. Hinton asked for an example of a language pattern used in poetry, Colson replied, "Figurative language." The teacher responded, "Figurative language. Sure. And why do we use figurative language?" Colson answered that figurative language was used "to describe pictures in our head." The teacher followed up by asking, "Who can name a kind of figurative language that you might see in a poem?" Various students then were able to name and define similes and metaphors as figurative language. The students also provided examples of each type of figurative language, such as "The sun is as bright as a light bulb," and "The frog is as flat as a pancake."

After the activation of students' prior knowledge about poetry, the teacher directed students' attention to their homework, which included preparing to perform a poem the next day. The teacher explained that students would be given a packet of twenty-seven poems. During class students would read all the poems independently and select three. From the three they chose, they would select one poem to perform in class the following day. The teacher then explained that whenever she read poems aloud to the class, it was a type of performance. She then modeled reading a poem aloud from the text *Where the Sidewalk Ends* by Shel Silverstein (1974). The teacher asked students to listen carefully and observe her performance as she read the poem.

Enter This Deserted House

But please walk softly as you do.
Frogs dwell here, and crickets do too.

Ain't no ceiling, only blue.
Jays dwell here, and sunbeams too.

Floors are flowers–take a few.
Ferns grow here and daises do too.

Whoosh, swoosh–tu-wit, tu-woo.
Bats dwell here and hoot owls too.

Ha-ha-ha, hee-hee, hoo-hoooo,
Gnomes dwell here and goblins too.

And my child, I thought you knew,
I dwell here. . . and so do you.

Ms. Hinton read the poem with prosody, including expression, intonation, and phrasing. When she asked students what they noticed as she read the poem, Caitlin replied, "You paused and there were short sentences and long sentences so that you would pause and then do a . . . long sentence and a pause and do a short sentence . . ." Ms. Hinton asked students what element in the poem indicated where she should pause as she read. She showed students the print version of the poem as she circulated through the room. Again, Caitlin noted, "There are those dashes in there," referring to the punctuation contained in the poem. The teacher replied, "There are some dashes. Okay. And lines. And at the end, see the dot-dot-dot? It's within the same sentence, but that told me to take a pause there."

    The teacher then asked whether her students would consider her reading aloud of the poem a performance. Most of the students replied yes. She reiterated by saying, "What did I say about poems? They really need to be? *Read out loud to hear them*. So that is what you are going to practice doing."

Ms. Hinton then read "Ickle Me, Pickle Me, Tickle Me Too" (Silverstein 1974) aloud with prosody, including expression, intonation, and phrasing.

> Ickle Me, Pickle Me, Tickle Me too,
> Went for a ride in a flying shoe,
> "Hooray!"
> "What fun!"
> "It's time we flew!"
> Said Ickle Me, Pickle Me, Tickle Me too.
>
> Ickle was captain and Pickle was crew
> And Tickle served coffee and mulligan stew
> As higher
> And higher
> And higher they flew,
> Ickle Me, Pickle Me, Tickle Me too.
>
> Ickle Me, Pickle Me, Tickle Me too,
> Over the sun and beyond the blue.
> "Hold on!"
> "Stay in!"
> "I hope we do!"
> Cried Ickle Me, Pickle Me, Tickle Me too.
>
> Ickle Me, Pickle Me, Tickle Me too
> Never returned to the world they knew,
> And nobody
> knows what's
> happened to
> Dear Ickle Me, Pickle Me, Tickle Me too.

Once the teacher stopped reading, a student commented that while the teacher read, "I think you made some things softly and then louder and louder." Ms. Hinton again noted the usefulness of punctuation when reading poetry, "Okay, and it's because I had exclamation points so I—what does it mean? It's got to be loud. It's got to have some punch."

In addition to underscoring the importance of punctuation in the performance of poetry, Ms. Hinton also highlighted the importance of intonation. "Listen to this line again, '*And Tickle served coffee and Mulligan stew As higher, and higher, and higher they flew.*'" As she reread the line from the poem, she used her hand to indicate that her pitch was rising as she read. She then asked, "What did you hear? How did it sound?" A student responded, "Like someone was jumping up higher and higher." Ms. Hinton redirected students back to her voice, "What was my voice doing?" as she reread the line again. A student replied that the teacher's voice was getting louder. Ms. Hinton replied, "Well, not—I wasn't getting louder. What was happening to my voice? Think of music. Was my pitch getting higher? You know, like you could talk like this, really high. Or you could talk like this, very low. So because the poem was saying 'Higher, and higher, and higher' your voice takes the listener up with you. So that is something you will have to practice with your poems." As she explained intonation to students, Ms. Hinton used the pitch of her voice to demonstrate the ability to get really high and really low with the pitch of your voice, based on what the poet wrote.

Ms. Hinton read aloud a third poem by Silverstein (1974) in order to demonstrate the ability to get really high and really low with the pitch of your voice. As she transitioned from the second to the third poem, she said, "Let's do another funny poem. Now we did a poem about cats for Caitlin. 'My Dog is Too Friendly'—this poem is for Jeffery." Several times throughout the lesson, the teacher attempted to draw Jeffery into the lesson, but he had not responded.

After the teacher read the third poem aloud, modeling fluency, she closed the lesson by reviewing what students were to do during the remainder of the class. She reminded students that they were to read all of the poems in the packet and select three that they might like to perform. The teacher then asked students to repeat the directions and the goal for the class period: "Who can tell me what they're going to have within the hour? Arzou?" Arzou responded, "We have to find three poems that we want to perform." The teacher answered, "Three poems you want to perform. All right. So tonight, these three poems, you are going to practice. And how should you practice?" One student replied that they should read the poems out loud to themselves. The teacher replied, "You're going to practice it by yourself. Where do you think you should practice it?" A student stated that they should practice reading their poems "in front of a mirror." Ms. Hinton then said, "In front of a mirror. And then what do you think maybe you could do?" Another student answered, "I don't know. Practice in front of someone else?" The teacher said, "In front of somebody. Choose someone in your family to practice in front of."

As the students began reading independently the poems in their packets, Ms. Hinton attended to individual questions and assignments and then, once everyone was settled, met with small groups for spelling and guided reading at the back table. She saved the last few minutes of class to review the poetry assignment: "Anyone have questions about the poetry homework for tonight?" When Tamika asked if they had to read all three, Ms. Hinton responded, "No, you're going to read one, but you better practice all three because I get to pick the one." The following day, Ms. Hinton gave feedback on children's performances.

QUESTIONS

1. Did Ms. Hinton devote adequate instructional time to modeling fluency by reading the poems aloud? Did she model too many or too few poems? Was her modeling of prosodic reading adequate? Provide examples to support your answers.
2. Why did Ms. Hinton focus on reading fluency in this lesson? Do you think that is a wise choice? Why or why not?
3. What are some fluency techniques that Ms. Hinton used to engage her students during this lesson?

Commentary on Case 2: A Teacher Educator's Perspective

Rose Marie Codling

The case of Mrs. Hinton's poetry lesson demonstrates several effective practices with respect to reading fluency instruction. Mrs. Hinton carefully previews and selects appropriate materials to use during the lesson. She is aware of the aspects of fluency she wishes to emphasize and chooses poems that will enable her to highlight those aspects. In this case, she wanted the students to utilize punctuation and to notice how the author's word choice implied changes in intonation. Her choice of poems accomplished this objective nicely.

Mrs. Hinton uses read-aloud as a vehicle for the lesson, which is a most effective way to model oral reading fluency. An extension of this practice might be to also model disfluency. That is, she might have read a selection to students in a slow, halting, or monotone manner, encouraging them to evaluate her oral reading. Students are quick to provide feedback—"Read faster!" "It sounds too boring!" Read-aloud provides the teacher with an excellent way to model appropriately paced, smooth oral reading.

35

Educators are becoming increasingly aware of the connection between fluency and comprehension. Mrs. Hinton's actions demonstrate an understanding of this important link. She begins by activating the students' background knowledge about poetry forms and language structures. She reviews previously taught lessons to prompt students to think about what they already know about poetry. Additionally, Mrs. Hinton has students read a wide array of poems in the poetry packet and has them repeatedly read the three poems they may perform. Wide, nonrepetitive reading and rereading are both strong, research-supported practices for improving fluency and comprehension (Kuhn 2005; Kuhn and Stahl 2003).

Mrs. Hinton especially relies on the strategy of rereading. This strategy is appropriate in this case for several reasons. First, any oral reading performance should be supported by rehearsals to increase students' motivation and reduce anxiety. Second, multiple readings of the same piece allow students to focus first on word decoding issues that may arise, then on comprehension of the material, and finally on the oral rendition in the performance. Third, poetry often contains nonsense words, colloquialisms, or figurative language that can provide a stumbling block to comprehension, especially for second language learners. The opportunity to read the materials multiple times is critical for these students to assure comprehension prior to their performance.

In sum, teachers should consider several factors in planning fluency instruction. First, careful selection of the materials is essential. Second, teacher modeling of good fluency demonstrates the concept and enables students to see its importance. Finally, it is critical to use research-based techniques to maximize the impact of instruction on both fluency and comprehension.

Case 3

Developing Vocabulary Knowledge through Explanation of Words in Context

Fifth-Grade Reading Lesson

CASE SETTING

Leslie Gabriel taught these lessons at Brookfield Elementary School during a ninety-minute class period
in mid-May. During this time, Ms. Gabriel taught three
small groups. While the small reading groups met at a
large square table at the back of her spacious room, the
other students worked independently on related assignments at individual desks arranged in groups of four. A
veteran teacher of thirty-five years, Ms. Gabriel had a
class of twenty-five students with a wide range of reading
levels. About one-third of her students were currently or
had previously been in ESOL, more than half were or had

been on FARMs, and at least seven were or had been on
an IEP. The class was also culturally diverse: 37 percent
were Hispanic, 37 percent White, 16 percent African
American, and 10 percent Asian. This case details the vocabulary instruction that Ms. Gabriel provided in two of
these groups. Ms. Gabriel met with the first group from
approximately 9:45 to 10:15, and the second group from
approximately 10:15 to 10:40. The four students in the
first group were reading on a fourth grade level and had
IEPs. The nine students in the second group were reading on a fifth grade reading level. At the beginning of the
year, most of these students had been reading on a third
grade level. Both groups contained ESOL students who
were born in countries other than the United States, and
whose native language was not English.

CASE OVERVIEW

In this case, Ms. Gabriel actively engaged her students in
instructional conversations designed to explain the meaning of the vocabulary words in context of the texts they
had read (Blachowicz and Fisher 2000). She worked a
great deal on leading her students to an understanding of
vocabulary words to comprehend texts. The first group
was reading a realistic fiction text, *Justin and the Best
Biscuits in the World* (Walter 1986), whereas the second
group was reading a science fiction text, *The Green Book*
(Walsh 1982). Prior to their small group instruction, the
students in each group read chapters in their respective
texts and selected words that they didn't understand

(Fisher, Blachowicz, and Smith 1991). Based on common misunderstandings, Ms. Gabriel chose vocabulary words for her students to learn, and they completed concept of definition maps (Schwartz and Rafael 1985) on these words. During small group instruction, Ms. Gabriel supported her students' understanding of these words through instructional conversations that explained the meaning of the words in the context of the texts they had read and in the context of the sentences they had written (Wilkinson and Silliman 2000). Both groups were learning to use context as a clue to the meaning of a word or phrase, a Common Core Standard. However, the complexity of their texts differed from a story about everyday experiences to experiences distinctly different from children's lives. Ms. Gabriel had an easy rapport with students, and she regularly gave them positive reinforcement and encouragement.

RELATED COMMON CORE STATE STANDARD

Grades 3–5
Language
Standard 4:

- Determine or clarify the meaning of unknown and multiple-meaning words and phrases based on grade 3–5 reading and content, choosing flexibly from a range of strategies.
- Use context (e.g., cause/effect relationships and comparisons in text) as a clue to the meaning of a word or phrase.

THE CASE

Ms. Gabriel began the reading/language arts block by explaining the day's reading assignments to the whole class. She had work for three reading groups listed on the board. Ms. Gabriel expected her students to work independently at their desks while she conducted small group instruction.

Vocabulary Instruction for Students Reading Below Grade Level

Ms. Gabriel called the first small group to a large table in the back of the classroom. The four students in this group had read a chapter in *Justin and the Best Biscuits in the World*. Ms. Gabriel began the lesson by identifying the problem in the assigned chapter. Then she and her students talked about the following vocabulary words: *scattered*, *strained*, *bonus*, *rescued*, and *retorted*. She had these words posted on chart paper. As Ms. Gabriel's students reported on these words, they referenced their completed vocabulary webs. They had completed one web for each vocabulary word. Each web had a circle in the center for the vocabulary word and additional circles and rectangles branching out from the center circle that contained a sentence from the text, a definition, synonyms, antonyms, the part of speech, and a student-composed sentence (see Figure 3.1).

Ms. Gabriel asked Jackie to read the sentence from the text that contained the word *scattered*. Jackie read, "Only a few girls were scattered about." Ms. Gabriel explained that this sentence referred to girls on a playground. She continued, "I want you to think about the playground

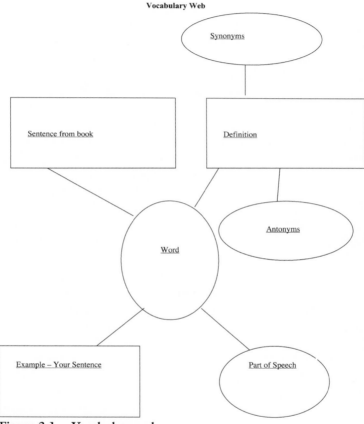

Figure 3.1. Vocabulary web.

and think what it would look like if you saw girls scattered about." Then she prompted Jackie to read her definition of scattered. Jackie responded, "To move or be made to move in many different directions."

After Jackie stated her definition, Ms. Gabriel asked, "So do you think there were a lot of girls all together on the playground? Do you think there were, Eduardo? Were all the girls all together on the playground, if they're scattered all about?" Eduardo responded, "Yeah." As she moved close to Gina, Ms. Gabriel asked "Are we, are Gina and I scattered?" Eduardo responded, "No." Ms. Gabriel confirmed his response and asked, "What are we?" Eduardo replied, "Together." Ms. Gabriel confirmed, "We're together. Suppose I walk over here. [Ms. Gabriel walked away from the group.] Are we still together?" "No," Eduardo said. Ms. Gabriel agreed, "We're more scattered. If you look at our tables, are our teams all together?" Several students answered, "No." Ms. Gabriel asked, "What's another word to describe the way our teams are arranged?" Eduardo responded, "Scattered." Ms. Gabriel stated, "They're scattered in different parts. So we said that the word *scattered* means in different places on the playground. There probably weren't a lot of girls, and they were all over the playground, scattered." Ms. Gabriel concluded this instructional conversation by asking Jackie to read her self-composed sentence.

Ms. Gabriel moved onto the next vocabulary word on the list, *strained*. She said, "Gina, say the word for me." Gina said, "Strange." Ms. Gabriel corrected her, "Strained," emphasizing the *ed* ending. Ms. Gabriel asked, "Can you say it again?" Gina replied, "Stranged." Once again, Ms. Gabriel repeated the word, "Strain-ed."

Ms. Gabriel asked Gina to read the sentence from the text that contained the word *strained*. Gina read aloud, "Hydia, his younger sister, strained under bags of groceries as she removed them from the car." Ms. Gabriel said, "Hydia strained under bags of groceries. Now, I don't have bags of groceries, but I do have these books. Feel these books. What would you say they are?" Gina responded, "Heavy." Ms. Gabriel continued, "Let's say I had these books, plus those books, plus two of your notebooks, and I'm trying to walk. What would you say about this? I'm straining. Why would I be straining?" Gina said, "Because they are heavy." Ms. Gabriel then asked Gina to read her definition. Gina said, "Not natural or forced." Ms. Gabriel responded, "Forced. So if I'm straining, it's not natural. It's real heavy, and it's forced."

Then Ms. Gabriel prompted Gina to read her self-composed sentence. Gina said, "She had a stranged look." Ms. Gabriel said, "That's it! She [Gina] thinks the word is strange. The word is not strange. It's like if I looked at you like, heh? That's a strange look. The word *strained* is something that maybe you're forced to do. For example, if I had to run twenty-five miles right now, it would strain me a lot. It would put a lot of pressure and be very difficult for me."

Following her explanation, Ms. Gabriel called on Latitia to read her self-composed sentence. Latitia said, "The girls strained to carry the laundry basket down the steps." Ms. Gabriel praised Latitia, "Very good. And you modeled it after the sentence that was in the book."

Ms. Gabriel had the group go to the next vocabulary word on the list, *bonus*. She called on Latitia to read from the text. Latitia read, "I had a wonderful sale today. That means a big bonus." Ms. Gabriel repeated the sentences, and then related the word *bonus* to a more concrete and relevant example, bonus questions in math or reading.

Ms. Gabriel asked Eduardo to read the sentence from text corresponding to the word *rescued*. Eduardo read, "Justin smiled and sighed. At last his mother had rescued him, as she always did." Ms. Gabriel continued, "So if you rescue someone, what do you do, Eduardo?" He replied, "Set free from danger." Ms. Gabriel repeated Eduardo's response and asked, "Was Justin in danger when Mother rescued him?" Eduardo thought he was. Ms. Gabriel continued, "You think so? Well, let's say I'm out in the ocean, and I don't have a flotation device, and a shark is coming towards me. And you went to rescue me. You're really getting me out of danger, aren't you? Was Justin's mother getting him out of danger?" Eduardo replied, "No." Ms. Gabriel confirmed his response and asked, "How was she rescuing him then? Jackie?" Jackie responded, "She was helping him." "Right," Ms. Gabriel said. "She was helping him because who was yelling at him?" Jackie responded, "Evelyn." Ms. Gabriel confirmed that Evelyn was yelling at Justin and asked, "So she was really helping him get out of trouble, wasn't she?" Eduardo responded, "Uh-huh."

Then Ms. Gabriel asked Eduardo to read his self-composed sentence that contained the word *rescued*. Eduardo read, "My mom rescued me from my sister." Ms. Gabriel asked the group if that was a good sentence. Most students responded that it was an okay sentence. When Ms. Gabriel asked Jackie why she thought it was just okay, Jackie responded, "Because it needs more." Ms. Gabriel said, "I want to know what was happening." Speaking to Eduardo, Ms. Gabriel said, "My mother rescued me from my sister when . . . Look at me and tell me. What was your sister doing to you?" Eduardo replied, "Hitting me." Ms Gabriel replied, "That's it. My mother rescued me from my sister when she was hitting me."

Ms. Gabriel moved on to the final vocabulary word on the list, *retorted*. Ms. Gabriel asked Latitia to read the sentence from the book. Latitia read, "You, Evelyn retorted." Ms. Gabriel repeated the sentence with enunciation and expression. Then she asked, "So just from listening to that, what did you think it meant?" Latitia responded, "She [Evelyn] answered back harshly." "Okay," said Ms. Gabriel. "You think it has something to do with her answer." Ms. Gabriel asked Latitia to read her definition. Latitia read, "To answer back harshly." Ms. Gabriel continued, "So if I said, 'Oh, you,' would I have retorted then?" Latitia responded, "No." Ms. Gabriel continued, "If I said, 'You!' What did I do?" Latitia replied, "You retorted." Ms. Gabriel confirmed her answer.

Ms. Gabriel then asked Latitia to read her self-composed sentence. Latitia said, "My sister was being so retorted." Aware that Latitia had confused the word *retorted* with the word *retarded*, Ms. Gabriel said to the group "Listen to what she [Latitia] said. 'My sister was being so retorted.'" Then, Ms. Gabriel prompted Latitia to compose another sentence and to model it after the sentence in the text. Addressing Latitia, Ms. Gabriel said, "Read the sentence in the book." Latitia read, "You, Evelyn retorted." Ms. Gabriel responded, "All right. So you need 'Evelyn retorted.'" Ms. Gabriel continued, "Come here! Ms. Gabriel re . . ." "Torted," finished Latitia. Ms. Gabriel provided another sentence for Latitia to complete. Ms. Gabriel said, "Sit down!" "Ms. Gabriel retorted," finished Latitia.

When Ms. Gabriel and her students finished reporting on the five vocabulary words, they worked together on matching the five words with their definitions. The students completed the task accurately. Then Ms. Gabriel continued the lesson by answering and discussing comprehension questions that related to the chapter.

Vocabulary Instruction for Students Reading on Grade Level

Ms. Gabriel called the second small group to the large table in the back of the classroom. The nine students in this group had read a chapter in *The Green Book* (Walsh 1982). Ms. Gabriel began this lesson by reviewing the various reading strategies her students employed when reading the assigned chapter. Then she and her students discussed the following vocabulary words: *calculator*, *gravity*, *exploration*, *minimum*, *destination*, *cubicle*, *flabby*, *technology*, and *disaster*. She had written these words on a chalkboard. As Ms. Gabriel's students reported on these words, they referenced their completed vocabulary webs.

Ms. Gabriel asked Kyle to read the sentence from the text that contained the word *calculator*. After Kyle read the sentence, he offered his definition. Then, continuing to ask students to read from their concept of definition maps, Ms. Gabriel asked her students to name synonyms for the word *calculator*. She noted that it could be difficult to think of synonyms for *calculator*, noting, "I'm thinking maybe in a grocery store, they have those adding machines. What would be the opposite of using a calculator?" Her students answered, "Your mind." "By hand."

Ms. Gabriel concluded their instructional conversation of *calculator* by inviting Kyle to share his self-composed sentence. Kyle read, "In math class you use a calculator to solve math problems." Ms. Gabriel said, "Very good. You related it to something we do."

Ms. Gabriel moved to the next vocabulary word on the list, *gravity*. She asked Saul to read the sentence from the text that contained the word. Saul said, "That's just the ship's gravity machine." Then Ms. Gabriel explained that because gravity does not exist in space, the characters in the text had a gravity machine on their spaceship. To support her students' understanding of gravity, Ms. Gabriel asked, "What would the gravity machine do?" Daniel responded, "Make them feel how it was on Earth." Ms. Gabriel replied, "Exactly. It would be hard for them to fly around for four years. Wouldn't it? And so they had a gravity machine on the ship so that they would be able to move around like they might do on Earth."

After explaining the importance of the gravity machine on the spaceship, Ms. Gabriel asked, "What does the word *gravity* mean, Saul?" He replied, "The natural force that causes smaller objects to move towards the center of the Earth." Ms. Gabriel affirmed Saul's definition and restated it by saying, "In other words, it's what holds us down, isn't it?"

To confirm her students' understanding of gravity, Ms. Gabriel asked them, "If I let go of a feather and I [blowing sound], what's going to happen to the feather?" Through an instructional conversation, Ms. Gabriel and her students established that the feather would float gradually to the ground due to gravity. Ms. Gabriel summarized the conversation by stating, "It [the feather] will eventually come to the Earth."

Immediately following this conversation, Sergio inquired about why a helium balloon floats in the air, seemingly defying gravity. Ms. Gabriel responded to his question by asking, "Now, why does it [a helium balloon] float? What do you know about helium? Does anybody know anything about helium?" When another student outside of the group answered Ms. Gabriel's question, she acknowledged his response and repeated it for the group to hear. Then, she explained, "It [helium] is lighter than air so it would cause something to stay up in the air." From this explanation, Ms. Gabriel's students inferred that because helium is lighter than air, it causes the helium balloon to stay up in the air, seemingly defying gravity.

After Ms. Gabriel's students offered a synonym and an antonym for the word *gravity*, Ms. Gabriel directed the conversation to the next word, *exploration*. She asked Sergio to read the sentence from the text that contained *exploration*. Sergio read, "Our computer was intended for exploration journeys, not for colonization." Before explaining the word *exploration*, Ms. Gabriel directed Sergio's attention to the word *colonization* by asking, "You heard that word, *colonization*, before?" After Sergio responded with, "Uh-huh." Ms. Gabriel asked, "And where? In social studies?" She continued, "So they're [characters in the text] doing like our explorers did. They're [characters in the text] colonizing. They have to go and be colonists, like we read about at the very beginning of the year. So, what does it mean? What does exploration mean, Sergio?"

After Sergio shared his lengthy definition, Ms. Gabriel stated, "Give me the important part. *Exploration* is what?" Sergio said, "Discovery." Ms. Gabriel repeated his response and said, "It's going to a place, maybe where nobody has been, and you're going to discover new things." Then Ms. Gabriel asked Sergio to supply a synonym and antonym for exploration. Sergio offered *discovery* and *stationary*, respectively. After Ms. Gabriel verified his responses, she concluded the instructional conversation by asking Sergio to read his self-composed sentence that contained the word *exploration*.

After Ms. Gabriel and her students reported on the words *minimum* and *destination*, they reported on the word *cubicle*. Ms. Gabriel explained that the word *cubicle* made her think about people working in small spaces. She asked, "Have you ever seen that? At your parents' offices or anything?" Daniel replied, "Yeah." Ms. Gabriel continued, "They're not totally alone, but they're in a little section." Then Ms. Gabriel asked Daniel to read the sentence from the text that contained the word *cubicle*. Daniel read, "At first everyone hated it. They grumbled all the time about tiny cubicles." To support Daniel's understanding of *cubicle*, Ms. Gabriel explained that a cubicle is a small space, similar to his suggested synonyms of "tent" and "sleeping compartment."

Ms. Gabriel and her students reviewed the remaining vocabulary words of *flabby*, *technology*, and *disaster*, reporting information from their completed vocabulary webs. Then Ms. Gabriel continued the lesson by discussing personal, survival, and emotional needs and completing a corresponding graphic organizer.

QUESTIONS

1. To teach vocabulary words, Ms. Gabriel used the same instructional approach with both small groups of students. How would you characterize her approach?

2. Compare the two groups of students. How do the differences between these two groups affect the instructional conversations that Ms. Gabriel had with her students?

3. Compare Ms. Gabriel's approach to teaching vocabulary with Ms. Hinton's approach to teaching vocabulary. How are they similar or different?

4. What evidence do you see that Ms. Gabriel's instructional approach is particularly appropriate for students learning English? How might Ms. Hinton's approach, though different, be equally effective?

Case 4
Reading Strategies that Support Comprehension

Fifth-Grade Reading Lesson

CLASS SETTING

This lesson was taught by Jason DiLoretto at Ella Flagg Young Elementary School. Mr. DiLoretto was in his sixteenth year of teaching. The lesson took place in late spring. There were approximately twenty-five students in the class.

CASE OVERVIEW

Mr. DiLoretto began the lesson by facilitating a whole class discussion on *The Borning Room* (Fleischman 1991) in which his students summarized the important events in the chapters they previously read (Doctorow, Wittrock, and Marks 1978; NRP 2000). Next, Mr. DiLoretto read out loud and facilitated another whole class discussion on the protagonist's character traits. During this read aloud and discussion, Mr. DiLoretto modeled and prompted his students to employ several different reading strategies, including activating prior knowledge, making connections, questioning, inferring, and predicting (Morrow, Wamsley, Duhammel, and Fittipaldi 2002; NRP 2000). Then Mr. DiLoretto had his students form two literature discussion groups (Daniels 2002; NRP 2000). One group discussed *Ben Franklin of Old Philadelphia* (Cousins 1952), and the other group discussed *The Root Cellar* (Lunn 1985). After each group summarized the important events in their respective texts, each group identified character traits of the protagonists in these texts. Mr. DiLoretto guided his students in their discussions as they employed various reading strategies (Cazden 1988; Morrow et al. 2002). Regardless of whether the instruction was teacher-led or occurred in small groups, students repeatedly referred to details in the text to describe how characters in the story responded to challenges and to summarize the text, a Common Core Standard.

RELATED COMMON CORE STATE STANDARD

Grades 4–5
Reading Literature
Standard 2:

- Determine a theme of a story, drama, or poem from details in the text, including how characters in a story or drama respond to challenges or how the speaker in a poem reflects upon a topic.
- Summarize the text.

THE CASE

Whole Class Discussion: Plot

Mr. DiLoretto began the lesson by asking his students to summarize the main events in *The Borning Room* (Fleischman 1991). He asked, "Who can summarize the main events in *The Borning Room*? The five or six most important events . . . If I were to hand out a storyboard, which events would you choose? In chronological order?"

One student suggested "The first main event is they described the borning room where she was actually born." Mr. DiLoretto urged the student to continue. "Can you describe it for us? Could you paint a picture of *The Borning Room* for us in words?" The student described the room as "a room with a plaid quilt on the bed, a table with a lamp, and a Bible. And a sink in the corner."

Another student suggested the second main event was "when she's born." Mr. DiLoretto responded with a question. "Who is she? Who are we talking about?" A student answered, "Georgina." The teacher inquired about the next main event.

Another student described the third event as "when the mom died and the one boy died and the other boy was born at the same time." For clarification this student added, "The first baby that came out was dead, and there was still another one alive inside."

Finally, Mr. DiLoretto suggested there was another important event to mention. "When the grandfather died?" offered Eli. Mr. DiLoretto agreed. "And why was it such an important event, Eli, to mention that grandfather passed away?" Eli responded, "Because he was the first person to die in the book?" Mr. DiLoretto agreed but asked, "But also he had a very close relationship with whom?" Several students answered, "Georgina." "Yeah, she really looked up to him, did she not?" the teacher added. "She spent time with him in the woods, noticing things that most people might not notice like the birds and the different types of trees." Briefly, Mr. DiLoretto made the point that young people today spend more time with indoor activities than they do noticing nature. "How many people . . . take the time each day to notice the birds and the different types of trees?" One girl said she watches birds sometimes with her cat, but most of the students admitted they do not pay much attention to nature.

The discussion of the text's main events concluded with students noting two things. First, diphtheria was "causing people to die." Second, a character named Lucille got married. Mr. DiLoretto added "Who is that, now? That would be her sister. And who did she marry? Does anybody remember?" A student replied, "The Swedish guy."

Whole Class Discussion: Character Traits

After the students summarized the main events, Mr. DiLoretto announced, "I'd like to focus on character traits today." At this point, he walked to the closet, took out a laminated chart, and clipped it to the front board. This chart listed approximately thirty character traits. Mr. DiLoretto reminded his students that they had learned about character traits earlier in the year, and stated that the chart should be review. "You all have character traits, right? You sure do. Well, I would like to identify during our read aloud today some of Georgina's character traits."

Mr. DiLoretto continued, "Character traits are long lasting. They're with you from the time you're born probably until the time you die. But unfortunately fifth graders [and] some sixth graders confuse character traits with feelings." Mr. DiLoretto elaborated. "Upset, frustrated, joyful, sad, these are all some of the feelings that Georgina was experiencing . . . throughout the story. But these are not character traits because you can be sad one moment and be feeling joyful the next." Mr. DiLoretto said that he wanted the students to think about the difference between Georgina's character traits and feelings during the read aloud.

To further remind his students of the concept of character traits, Mr. DiLoretto made connections to a math lesson that he taught earlier in the day. This math lesson focused on attributes of a triangle, as well as the students' attributes and their families' attributes. Many of Mr. DiLoretto's students who participated in this reading lesson had also participated in his math lesson.

Mr. DiLoretto asked a student who was in a different math class to explain attributes. When this student seemed uncertain, Mr. DiLoretto asked a student from his own math class to explain attributes. "I think they're like character traits but . . . they describe a personality." Mr. DiLoretto agreed that character traits and attributes were similar in that they could both describe a personality, but he said there was also a difference between them. "We could also be talking about physical attributes, can't we? What are some of your physical attributes?" Then

Mr. DiLoretto asked, "What color are your eyes?" After the student answered, Mr. DiLoretto asked, "What color is your hair?" and "How tall are you?" The student continued to answer. Mr. DiLoretto concluded, "These are some of your physical attributes." He then turned to the class and asked, "Are physical attributes and character traits the same?" The students said, "No." Then Mr. DiLoretto asked his students to share some of their personal attributes. One student said he was funny. Mr. DiLoretto responded, "That could be an attribute. Absolutely." Another student said he was "athletic." Mr. DiLoretto agreed, "That's definitely a good attribute."

Mr. DiLoretto went on to say that during the math lesson he taught earlier in the day, the students named some of the attributes of a triangle. He then asked the students who were not in his math class, "What do you think some of those attributes were of the triangle?" One student stated, "It has three sides." Another student said a triangle had vertices. A third student said a triangle had three angles. A fourth student said, "All the angles add up to 180." Mr. DiLoretto inquired about the units. "Degrees," said the student. "Oh, you guys are really good," responded Mr. DiLoretto. "These are some of the same attributes that my math class gave me."

Returning to the reading lesson, Mr. DiLoretto explained, "So I guess what I'm trying to do here [is] I'm trying to make the connection between attributes, which you're going to cover in math [and] . . . character traits, which we're going to cover in today's reading lesson. I'm making a connection from one subject [*math*] to the other [*reading*]."

Then the students spent some time making connections between themselves and the characters in *The Borning Room*. Mr. DiLoretto said he wanted his students to make connections between "what these characters are experiencing and feeling" and what they are experiencing and feeling. He also said he would ask his students to identify five of Georgina's character traits when he completed the read aloud.

Mr. DiLoretto noted, "I've heard some people talk to me about *The Borning Room* and say, you know, it's kind of a dark book. What do they mean when they say, 'It's kind of a dark book'?" The students pointed out some negative things that happened in the book, such as "people dying and the disease spreading around." However, the students also noted some positive things, including a wedding and the birth of some of Georgina's siblings. A student named Roshay noted, "Right after something positive happens, something bad happens." Then she predicted, "I think probably after they get . . . married, I bet that the husband and wife are going to die." Mr. DiLoretto sounded surprised. "That's a strong prediction you're making there, young lady."

Reading Aloud to the Whole Class

Before starting the read aloud, Mr. DiLoretto reviewed the recent events in *The Borning Room*. Then he asked his students to consider how Georgina was feeling during those events. Next he reread the section where Georgina talks with the teacher in her home. When he finished, a student described Georgina's feelings as "happy . . . because of the teacher, because he's staying in their house." Mr. DiLoretto asked the student, "Have you ever had the same happy, joyful feeling after meeting someone?" The student said she had experienced this feeling with her friend "Jessica because, well, at the beginning of the year I didn't know if she was going to be mean to me or something like that. But now she's my friend." Another student suggested that Georgina was feeling "shocked and surprised because . . . her friend had told her fortune that she'd meet someone and marry that person." Finally, a third student said Georgina was feeling "shy because she's a little timidly [sic] and stuff, maybe while she was talking because it says she blushed, too."

Then Mr. DiLoretto read aloud the section detailing how Georgina cared for her brother, Zeb, who was very ill. For several days Georgina stayed up with Zeb, and the teacher sometimes stayed up with her in the evenings playing chess. Georgina's Aunt Irna remarked that checkers would be a better game for a woman, and Mr. DiLoretto stopped and asked the students what they thought. "[Do] you agree with that, that girls can't handle the game of chess and that they should stick strictly to checkers, which is a lot easier? Do you agree with that, Bai?" The student disagreed, and Mr. DiLoretto asked for an explanation. "Because women are equal to men," said Bai. "You mean they can think the same way?" asked Mr. DiLoretto. Bai responded, "Uh-huh."

Mr. DiLoretto continued reading aloud from the text. He became animated with his hands and expressive with his voice as he read the text. The students were all listening attentively and seemed to enjoy the read aloud, which was a regular occurrence in Mr. DiLoretto's reading lessons. As he read, Mr. DiLoretto took time to look at the students. It seemed that he looked at them to put more emphasis on the story rather than to see if they were paying attention. In this part of the story, Zeb's condition worsened, and Georgina increased her determination to help him recover from his illness. The teacher crushed eggshells and put them down Zeb's throat, causing the membrane in his throat to break as he coughed to rid himself of the shells.

When Mr. DiLoretto finished the read aloud, a student remarked, "That was mostly all positive because he's recovering, everyone's recovering. Nobody died." Mr. DiLoretto added that Georgina's courtship with the teacher also began at the end of the section that he had just read.

Then Mr. DiLoretto asked, "Who can describe, give me one of Georgina's character traits? We've really gotten to know this young lady. Not only do I want you to give me a character trait, but I want you to give me an example from the story that would support the character trait that you've chosen to describe Georgina."

One student suggested that Georgina was confident, and Mr. DiLoretto asked her to elaborate. "Give me an example from the story where she shows that she's a confident young lady." The student described how Georgina was sure she would be able to save her brother, Zeb, from his illness. Another student suggested that Georgina was argumentative. "Argumentative?" asked Mr. DiLoretto. "You think that's one of her character traits? Give me an example from the story that would support that." The student explained, "Because she always argues with her aunt, like, you have to do this and she was like, no, I'm not. So

I think she was pretty argumentative with her." Another student seemed to agree that Georgina might have been argumentative, but he suggested, "That would be a feeling."

At this point, the students spontaneously began talking to one another. One student suggested that *argumentative* was a feeling rather than a trait: "Argumentative would be good because her aunt was annoyed doing that but she used to say okay to her mom and stuff but that would be a feeling." But all the other students persisted in explaining why they thought *argumentative* was a trait. One student compared Georgina's trait to someone she knew, saying, "My friend is like that. She thinks that she knows everything, and then she'll do something wrong and then like, she always [inaudible] because she doesn't like to tell her mom."

Mr. DiLoretto brought the conversation back to the text by asking, "Do you have another character trait that would describe our main character?" Lindsey described Georgina as "loving, because she loves Zeb and she takes care of him and she said that she almost raised him." Kien said Georgina was attentive. "She's like, she was always, like if somebody was sick she would always pay attention to them." The same boy who suggested that argumentative was a feeling also suggested attentive was a feeling because it would "not always be there." Mr. DiLoretto responded to the concern this time. He stated, "But her personality, she did show that she was attentive to the family and taking care of them and in that regard, that definitely could be one of her qualities. That's where I thought Kien was coming from with that." A third student described Georgina as proud that she had helped her brother survive his illness.

Literature Discussion Groups

At this point, Mr. DiLoretto sent his students to one of two student-led literature discussion groups. One group was reading *Ben Franklin of Old Philadelphia* (Cousins 1952); the other group was reading *The Root Cellar* (Lunn 1985). Mr. DiLoretto asked the students to summarize the chapters that they read over the weekend. He also asked them to generate answers to his question about the character traits of the protagonists in their respective texts, "just like I've modeled for you." Then Mr. DiLoretto added, "I want you to be able to give me examples that support the character trait that you've chosen." As the students began to work in their literature discussion groups, Mr. DiLoretto provided guidance as necessary.

Mr. DiLoretto started *The Root Cellar* group's discussion by asking, "What happened in *The Root Cellar*? I can't wait to hear. What happened in *The Root Cellar*?" He asked the group leader, Emmitt, to call on someone for an answer. Emmitt called on Zameer, who began detailing the events of the story: "Then she [Rose] starts cleaning everything off the thing and she finds boards, two board doors and she opens them, prying them open. And she goes down some steps . . ." After letting Zameer go on for a while longer, Mr. DiLoretto interrupted with "We don't want every detail. . . . These people should have read those chapters, Zameer. We just want the main parts."

Zameer tried again: "And then Rose meets Will who's playing, trying to talk to the birds and they have a conversation and then Susan comes back and they all talk and they keep thinking she's lost and they say, 'Are you from a schooner? Is your daddy a boat driver?'" This time another student in the group tried to insert more detail ("she still stayed with the dog") to which Zameer replied, "That's every detail."

Rather than resolving this disagreement, Mr. DiLoretto thanked Zameer and asked the students their feelings about the chapter, bringing the discussion back to character traits. One student said that Rose, the main character, was polite. Mr. DiLoretto asked for information from the text to support this inference. The student responded, "Well, when people like talk to her, like in a mean way or something. . . . She feels like, well, she just wants to talk nicely. She just agrees with whatever." Another student said that Rose was "selfish because . . . she doesn't really—all she thinks about is herself." Mr. DiLoretto asked for the student to elaborate. "Like her grandmother died. It didn't seem like she was really all sad and she was like, 'Oh, we have to go to relatives that I don't like.' And she was only thinking about herself." At this point, Mr. DiLoretto suggested there may be a contradiction. "Hmm," he said. "So one person says she's polite; the other says she's selfish. Wow. Help me out please. Bai? Have you been reading? Do you have a character trait that would describe Rose?"

Rather than pursuing the previous point, Mr. DiLoretto seemed to think it was more important to draw Bai into the discussion. Bai, who had been silent until now, responded, "I think she feels lonely." Before Mr. DiLoretto could finish asking for an example, Bai added, "Not like a feeling lonely, like she feels lonely in her heart. . . . Like she just wants to go home and she doesn't really know where her home is." Mr. DiLoretto seemed satisfied with the student's explanation that "lonely" could be a character trait. "Some people have that. And I like the way, if you were listening closely, tell them again how you supported that." Bai repeated himself. "She's like lonely in her heart. She doesn't know where she belongs." Another student suggested that Rose was responsible. "I think she's like responsible because when her grandmother died she called up the aunt. . . . Nobody told her to do that. She just did it on her own."

At this point, Mr. DiLoretto asked the students to begin reading the next three chapters in *The Root Cellar*. Before sending them back to their seats, he made a request. "Can you . . . come up with two, possibly three, new character traits while you're reading today that would describe Rose that we haven't already mentioned?"

Then Mr. DiLoretto addressed the *Ben Franklin of Old Philadelphia* group. "Did you have an opportunity to talk about some of Ben Franklin's character traits?" Roshay, the group leader, said they were still summarizing the main events. She was listing the main events as students suggested them, things like, "Ben Franklin . . . finally got a job . . . found out that many people in Philadelphia wore bright colors. . . . He's now a great letter writer." Roshay also used her leadership position to determine the final wording of the items on the list and to push for additional items, "Okay, we need one more."

Eager for the group to discuss character traits, Mr. DiLoretto helped Roshay change the topic of discussion. He said, "When they talk about . . . Ben Franklin's character traits, make sure that they're giving you examples from the story that would support that character trait and have your ears open, making sure it's a trait not a feeling."

When one student offered that Ben Franklin was helpful, Mr. DiLoretto immediately replied, "Give me an example from the story." The student explained, "He helped somebody out of the water," but the teacher asked for more detail. "Somebody was like in the water . . . and he pulled them out by the hair," added the student. Mr. DiLoretto asked, "He saved her life?" and suggested that courageous might be a character trait. "Also painful," said a student. Mr. DiLoretto corrected him. "Painful is a feeling, Trevor. That's what I want you to know the difference between."

The students continued to identify Ben Franklin's character traits and offer examples from the text to support their responses. "He's smart," said one student, "because he was really good in school, but his parents couldn't afford him to stay in school." Mr. DiLoretto requested the student use "a fifth grade word to describe [Ben Franklin], rather than use smart." The student changed his trait to "intelligent." Without pausing, another student said that Ben Franklin was also brave. Trevor argued that brave was a feeling. Mr. DiLoretto responded with, "Hmm. Brave could be a long-lasting quality, Trevor. You can be brave for your whole life, can't you?" Then he said, "Give me an example. I didn't hear her example." The student noted, "He was brave from running away." Another student suggested that he would have used the word adventurous to describe Ben Franklin running away because "he went on an adventure to New York City."

The students seemed eager to offer more character traits, but the lesson time ended. Mr. DiLoretto asked the group to return to their seats and to continue reading. Mr. DiLoretto ended the lesson by circulating around the classroom and making comments to individual students. "You're trying to catch up on your own, so you've got a lot of catching up to do. "That's great." "You're going to have a lot of fun doing that." "What's happening in your reading?" "What's happening in the story?" "What's one new thing you learned today?" "Are you understanding what you're reading?" "Make sure you have full understanding. I'm going to come back to you and ask that question. Make sure you understand what you're reading."

QUESTIONS

1. What did Mr. DiLoretto want his students to understand about character traits and attributes? Would you have made a similar connection? Why or why not?
2. Why did Mr. DiLoretto ask his students to support their character trait with examples from the text? How did he respond to the examples students gave? How would you have responded?
3. What did Mr. DiLoretto do to help students understand the difference between character traits and feelings? Would you have done anything differently?
4. When the students formed literature discussion groups, why did Mr. DiLoretto prompt them to summarize the important events in the texts prior to identifying the protagonists' character traits?
5. How did Mr. DiLoretto scaffold his students during their literature discussion groups?

Commentary on Case 4:
A Teacher's Perspective

Christine Peterson-Tardif

A t the beginning of the lesson, Mr. DiLoretto did an excellent job of bringing past knowledge to the front of the students' thinking. Another powerful strategy teachers can use is to have students generate a list of character traits. Can character traits ever change? Discuss past novels or readings that have a change in a character. The change happened over a long time, caused by an event or events. Later in the lesson Mr. DiLoretto talks about attributes. Then he asks a great thinking question, "Are physical attributes and character traits the same?" He did it again! He connected math to reading as he had connected reading to math in another lesson. Bravo!

During their book discussion, Mr. DiLoretto was helping students engage in a wonderful conversation about character traits. Students love to make connections to themselves and often will offer many, many, many examples of connections from a character or novel to their own lives. Be careful as a teacher to limit the connections. Have students cite examples from the text to support their statements. This directs the students to think about the characters in the book. Make a connection using the character instead of the student.

Another way to help Trevor with the concept of pain being a feeling would be to ask the question "What is a character trait?" This would direct Trevor to think of the difference between character traits and attributes. Does Trevor's definition of character trait describe pain? Make sure that you ask the same high-level questions of all levels of reading groups; don't jump to being explicit with lower-level readers, but spend the time helping them with thinking skills.

Commentary on Case 4: A Teacher Educator's Perspective

Rose Marie Codling

What strikes me most in Mr. DiLoretto's lesson is his concerted effort to scaffold students' learning. Based on the Vygotskian concept of the zone of proximal development, the assumption of instructional scaffolding is that a knowledgeable "other" is in a position to assist an individual's learning at just the right time, with the appropriate prompt or information. This entails knowing the students and providing challenge that is appropriate but not overwhelming.

To understand the concept of instructional scaffolding, an analogy to building construction is especially apt. When a building is being erected, a scaffold is built alongside the building at just the right height for workers to reach the current building level while enabling them to continue building to a higher level. A scaffold that is too tall will be ineffective for reaching the established portion of the building that needs to progress. A scaffold that is too short will not allow further construction upward. Instructional scaffolding is similar in that too much scaffolding means that students are not presented with any challenge that will further cognitive development and learning. Instructional scaffolding that is too limited will not provide students with the support necessary to handle intellectual tasks that they cannot handle independently.

Instructional scaffolding can take many forms (Clark and Graves 2004). Mr. DiLoretto appears to rely on three main scaffolding techniques. This scaffolding occurs during both a whole class read aloud and literature discussion groups.

Focused Questions

At times, Mr. DiLoretto responds with a direct question after a student speaks. These questions appear to be designed to elicit specific information to clarify what the student is saying or to identify specific text information.

Sample excerpt:
Another student suggested the second main event was "when she's born." Mr. DiLoretto replied with a question. "Who is she? Who are we talking about?"

Sample excerpt:
Finally, Mr. DiLoretto suggested there was another important event to mention. "When the grandfather died?" offered Eli. Mr. DiLoretto agreed. "And why was it such an important event, Eli, to mention that grandfather passed away?"

Requests for Explanation/Support from the Text

On several occasions, Mr. DiLoretto asks students to explain what they mean by a response or to provide information from the text that supports their contentions.

Sample excerpt:
One student suggested that Georgina was confident, and Mr. DiLoretto asked her to elaborate. "Give me an example from the story where she shows that she's a confident young lady."

Sample excerpt:
Another student suggested the character was argumentative. "Argumentative?" asked Mr. DiLoretto. "You think that's one of her character traits? Give me an example from the story that would support that." The student explained, "Because she always argues with her aunt, like, you have to do this and she was like, no, I'm not. So I think she was pretty argumentative with her."

Providing Relevant Information

There are times when it is clear from the students' responses that they do not understand an event or vocabulary word or have missed an important point. At these times, it is necessary for the teacher to directly provide the information that will facilitate students' continued engagement with the text.

Sample excerpt:
"Character traits are long lasting. They're with you from the time you're born probably until the time you die. But unfortunately fifth graders [and] some sixth graders confuse character traits with feelings." Mr. DiLoretto elaborated. "Upset, frustrated, joyful, sad, these are all some of the feelings that Georgina was experiencing . . . throughout the story. But these are not character traits because you can be sad one moment and be feeling joyful the next."

Sample excerpt:

When students were conflicted about character traits versus feelings, Mr. DiLoretto interjected, "But her personality, she did show that she was attentive to the family and taking care of them and in that regard, that definitely could be one of her qualities."

Sample excerpt:

When one student offered that Ben Franklin was helpful, Mr. DiLoretto immediately replied, "Give me an example from the story." The student explained, "He helped somebody out of the water," but the teacher asked for more detail. "Somebody was like in the water . . . and he pulled them out by the hair," added the student. Mr. DiLoretto asked, "He saved her life?" and suggested that courageous might be a character trait.

Although there are a number of ways for instructional scaffolding to occur, Mr. DiLoretto's use of scaffolding comes in the form of focused questions, requests for explanation/support from the text, and providing relevant information. Mr. DiLoretto begins by asking a broad question and his questions become more focused as the lesson progresses. He continually asks students to elaborate on or explain their answers using text support. Finally, he knows when it is appropriate to provide information to enable students to continue their discussion.

The case of Mr. DiLoretto provides three particular insights that might lead teachers to improve their use of instructional scaffolding. In short, Mr. DiLoretto knows his students well and he is aware of what they already know. Additionally, he clearly understands his content—the concept of character traits and how they are integral to comprehension of narrative text. Finally, he has developed insights about when to question, when to prompt, and when to explicitly provide information to facilitate students' engagement with text. These insights could become foci for improving instructional practice by novices and experienced teachers alike.

Case 5
Developing Personal
Connections to
Comprehend Text
Fifth-Grade Reading Lesson

CASE SETTING

This reading lesson was taught by Leslie Gabriel, a thirty-five-year veteran teacher, at Brookfield Elementary School on May 16. The reading block took place from 9:30 to 11:00 in a heterogeneous classroom setting. Within the reading block, Ms. Gabriel met with three small reading groups. This particular small group consisted of ethnically and linguistically diverse fifth grade students, reading on or above a fifth grade level. These students, some of whom had recently exited ESOL, were reading a text from the William and Mary program, a gifted and talented program. Ms. Gabriel met with this small group from approximately 10:40 to 11:20.

CASE OVERVIEW

This case demonstrates small group reading instruction where Ms. Gabriel taught and prompted her students to make personal connections to help them comprehend text (Anderson and Pearson 1984). Ms. Gabriel's extensive knowledge of her students helped her guide them to make those connections. Ms. Gabriel chose an autobiography, *The Lost Garden* (Yep 1996), so that when her students finished reading the text, they could write their own autobiographies. The scenario represents ways in which Ms. Gabriel motivated her students to read and understand a text (Guthrie and Wigfield 2000) by making personal connections to two aspects of story grammar: setting and characters (NRP 2000; Stein and Glenn 1979). Throughout, the teacher helped students build on one another's ideas, express themselves clearly, and both pose and respond to specific questions, a Common Core Standard.

RELATED COMMON CORE STATE STANDARD

Grades 3–5
Speaking and Listening
Standard 1:

- Engage effectively in a range of collaborative discussions (one-on-one, in groups, and teacher-led) with diverse partners on *grade 5 topics and texts*, building on others' ideas and expressing their own clearly.
- Pose and respond to specific questions by making comments that contribute to the discussion and elaborate on the remarks of others.

THE CASE

Ms. Gabriel began class by reviewing the day's reading assignments with the whole class. She had work for three small reading groups listed on the board. This reading group had read several chapters of *The Lost Garden*, an autobiography by a Chinese American who describes his exploration of personal identity growing up in a culturally diverse neighborhood. In preparation for this day's meeting, the students prepared graphic organizers that displayed Yep's feelings about his father's grocery store. Because Ms. Gabriel knew this group of students could handle the task, she had them design their own graphic organizer rather than complete a standard one. The other students in the class were expected to work independently at their desks while Ms. Gabriel worked with this small reading group.

Summarizing a Story's Plot and Characters

Ms. Gabriel began the lesson by having the students briefly summarize what they remembered about Yep's grandfather and father, especially what made life hard for his father. After the group established what Yep's father did for a living (i.e., worked in a restaurant and a gold mine; owned a grocery store) and who his friends were (i.e., Irish people), Ms. Gabriel said to the group, "Okay. You were to design a graphic organizer to show Yep's feelings about his father's grocery store." Asking students to share their organizers with the group, she called on Omar, who had his hand raised. "Okay, you want to show us? Just turn it around. You did a web, and you had feelings. What's the title of your web?" Omar answered, "Yep's Feelings About the Grocery Store," and then shared one reason why Yep liked the store: because his work there helped him improve in sports. When Ms. Gabriel asked how working in a grocery store could help a person be better at sports, Omar explained, "Because when he had to get the groceries that went on the high shelves, he started doing the top ladders, or the high ladder, and he would shoot it off the side and catch them." Ms. Gabriel pointed out that the specific sport Omar was talking about was basketball and suggested putting that in the graphic organizer.

Then Ms. Gabriel asked if another student had a different kind of graphic organizer. Carrie said she created a graphic organizer of the positive and negative things about the grocery store, and several students shared ideas that would fit in those categories, such as midnight snacks (positive) and cockroaches (negative). Ms. Gabriel wrote their answers on a large sheet of chart paper. When Carrie added that Yep liked the store because his chores helped him develop as a writer, Ms. Gabriel asked her to explain her thinking. Carrie offered that Yep had to be his own boss, set his own schedule, and interact with "many different people." "Absolutely," responded Ms. Gabriel, "and I bet he got a lot of characters for his books from what he saw. . . . Very good."

Analyzing the Importance of a Story's Setting

After exploring more aspects about working in the grocery store, Ms. Gabriel shifted the conversation to Yep's neighborhood and how it changed over the years. In preparation for this discussion, Ms. Gabriel asked her students to think about the changes in their own neighborhoods. Ms. Gabriel had a whiteboard next to her to list the students' ideas.

Ms. Gabriel began the discussion with, "It said that Yep's neighborhood changed over the years, but I asked you about your neighborhood. How many of you have seen changes in your neighborhood over the years? And I'd like to make a list of those changes because I think it's real important that as we live in an area for a while, and you guys haven't been living a long time, but what changes have you seen? Omar, give me one change." Omar said, "Neighbors move a lot." Ms. Gabriel responded, "That's a good one. Excellent. Would that affect you?" "Yeah," Omar responded. "Why?" asked Ms. Gabriel, "I agree." Omar said, "Because I had friends . . ." "And then they . . . ?" said Ms. Gabriel. "Left," answered Omar. "And then they moved," responded Ms. Gabriel, "Okay. Other changes that you notice about your neighborhood, something different?" The group went on to discuss home improvements, new homes being built, safety, and diversity. Anya commented, "In the past, kids would come out and probably ride their bikes more often, but now you don't really see a lot of people out." "Why is that?" asked Ms. Gabriel. "Probably because of the shootings," replied Anya.[1] "Okay, Oh, that's very good. So you don't see kids playing outside as much. Okay. That's an excellent one," said Ms. Gabriel.

---

1 There recently had been a series of shootings in the area. Schools and neighborhoods were told by the media and local government to take extra precautions.

Chapter Organizer

Novel: _____ Chapter: _____

Setting – Where/When

_____
_____
_____
_____
_____
_____
_____
_____

Characters

_____
_____
_____
_____

Main Events

1. _____
2. _____
3. _____
4. _____
5. _____

Vocabulary Word & Page

1. _____
2. _____
3. _____
4. _____
5. _____
6. _____
7. _____

Problem

_____
_____

Figure 5.1. Chapter organizer.

Then Emma offered, "Our town used to be all white and it isn't anymore." "Very good," said Ms. Gabriel, "So what word should I use to describe that? She said her town used to be all white and now it's not. So what's the word I can use to say that the neighborhood's become more what?" "Diverse," Emma said. Ms. Gabriel added "neighborhoods become more racially diverse" on the list.

"Now let me ask you, are these some of the things that happened in Yep's neighborhood too?" When several students answered, "Yes," Ms. Gabriel replied with, "Hopefully at this point you're really getting into this novel and you feel more comfortable about the setting and the characters." She then asked them to take out their graphic organizers for a specific chapter in the text. This graphic organizer included sections on setting and characters (see Figure 5.1).

Understanding Characters by Drawing Connections to Students' Qualities

The group finished their discussion of setting with a conversation about the importance of Chinatown to Yep's father and turned to the characters who were prominent in this chapter. Among other characters, the students described the grandmother, who had a good sense of humor and was fussy about food served in restaurants, and Momo, a kind, protective giant of a man.

Ms. Gabriel then asked students to look at a statement she had written on the board, "What made people most interesting was their imperfections. Their quirks were what made them unique and set them apart." Ms. Gabriel stated that the quote came directly from Yep in his book. She initiated a discussion about the meaning of that quote. She said, "Their quirks were what made them unique and set them apart. What does that mean? Their quirks. What is a quirk? Who can give me an example? Omar, give me one of your quirks that you think makes you more interesting." Students smiled and giggled at this personal turn in the lesson. Ms. Gabriel waited a few seconds and then said to Omar, "You want us to give you one?" "Yeah," Omar said. Ms. Gabriel called on Eric who looked eager to contribute, "He likes moving around." Ms. Gabriel expanded, "Okay. He likes moving around a lot. You never know where he's going to be and you often don't know what he's going to be doing. That's one of his quirks. Another one?" Carrie said, "Making weird sounds." "He often makes sounds," Ms. Gabriel said. She continued, "What's another one that really, to me, makes him very interesting? He's very outspoken, and he knows he has unbelievable background knowledge because he's been a lot of places, and he reads all the time. So, and he, Omar, you have a way of bringing something from wherever to a conversation. Would you agree that he does that?" Several students responded affirmatively. Ms. Gabriel continued, "He has a way of seeing things in a very special, unique way. Excellent. Now can you think about which ones get you in most trouble? He also wants to speak all the time. He's got so much to say that sometimes he doesn't have control about it. But it does make him interesting. He's one of those people you'll never forget." Larissa added, "And it's like he has a big imagination." Ms. Gabriel concurred, "He has a wonderful creative imagination. Okay. Now I want you to think of something about yourself. We did a good job on Omar. Let's pick someone else. Who'd be willing to have us give quirks about you?"

Students waved their hands high in the air, eager to have others discuss their quirks. "All right. Okay. Let's take a girl next. Let's take Larissa. What are some quirks that Larissa has that make her interesting and set her apart? I can tell you one. One is you speak through your nose, all the time. You know, like the other day, in the play, we were working on something and I was like, you know, you're and she goes, 'I talk like that all the time.' And I didn't realize it, but you do, don't you? You can't breathe through your nose." Larissa responded, "I can, but I don't like to." Ms. Gabriel said, "Have you ever heard anything like that? Talk about a quirk! And it gives her this well, when she was trying to create this character for the play; she used that so it's a very nasal thing. But it cracks me up because she's got this nay, you know, all the time. Other quirks about her?" Carrie responded, "She's very tall." "She's tall," said Ms. Gabriel, "Stands out tremendously because she's tall. She's always what?" Several students responded that she's always smiling. "She's always smiling. And it can be like in the play when something bad is supposed to happen," said Ms. Gabriel. Ms. Gabriel continued, "You know, and we're like, excuse me, that's not funny. You're not supposed to be happy there. And she can't help but smile. So those are some excellent quirks about her."

"Okay. Who else would be willing? Let's do Vee. He's got so many quirks. And they're so interesting. Chad?" Chad said, "He likes to do challenging math problems." Ms. Gabriel responded, "All right. I will talk about Vee the rest of my life. He walks in the room and he goes, 'Ms. Gabriel, did you know the mean of that chart?' or 'Ms. Gabriel, do you know those numbers are in the . . .' and I'm like, I didn't know that. His unbelievable ability in math certainly gets me. What else about him?" Larissa said, "He daydreams." "But it's the expressions that he makes on his face. You never know if he's happy or if he's not happy. And did you ever notice . . ." elaborated Ms. Gabriel. "He moves around a lot," said Larissa. "He can barely sit still," said Ms. Gabriel. Eric said, "He exaggerates." Ms. Gabriel agreed, "He exaggerates everything. Every movement. Every word. Everything."

Ms. Gabriel told the group that they had to stop because of the time. Several students were disappointed, a good indication that Ms. Gabriel had been successful in establishing student motivation and focus for their next meeting. She asked the students to turn in their graphic organizers and said that they would keep the quirks list up to work with at their next meeting.

QUESTIONS

1. Ms. Gabriel often used graphic organizers in her lessons. By comparing her three lessons described in this book, explain how Ms. Gabriel uses graphic organizers to differentiate for student learning.

2. A theory of metacognitive instruction is that teachers must explicitly describe reading strategies and explain when a reader would use them. Ms. Gabriel rarely uses metacognitive instruction, and yet the strategies that she teaches students are excellent.

What might be her rationale for not using meta-cognitive instruction? What might she do or say so that her instruction would be more metacognitive?

3. How does having explicit knowledge of students' personal lives demonstrate high-quality teaching?

4. In less expert hands, the discussions about changes in neighborhoods and personal quirks could be too personal and hurt children's feelings. Instead, Ms. Gabriel is able to use these discussions to help students understand the characters in the text better, to enhance student motivation, and to prepare for their own writing. How does she accomplish these outcomes?

Case 6
Modeling Reading Comprehension Strategies across Three Genres

Fifth-Grade Reading Lesson

CASE SETTING

This lesson was taught by Arthur Dunbar at Sandy Ridge Elementary School on March 30 from 2:15 to 3:25. The classroom was orderly with an overhead projector in the center of the room. Three student computers were in the back of the room and the teacher had a computer on his desk. The student desks were arranged in a U-shape and faced the blackboard in the front of the room. The students were a culturally diverse group of twenty-eight fifth graders.

CASE OVERVIEW

The following scenario was written from a reading lesson where fifth grade students were reviewing and using reading comprehension strategies. During the first part of the lesson, Mr. Dunbar reviewed and modeled previously taught reading comprehension strategies (Duffy, Roehler, Sivan, Rackliffe, Book, Meloth, et al. 1987). By modeling and reviewing these reading comprehension strategies using an expository text, Mr. Dunbar illustrated for his students the usefulness of interacting with text (National Reading Panel 2000; Pressley and Afflerbach 1995). During the second part of the lesson, Mr. Dunbar modeled and explained (Duffy et al. 1987) the new reading comprehension strategy of visualization (Gambrell and Bales 1986; Pressley 1976) with a narrative and a poem. This case illustrates a teacher working with his students to teach them comprehension strategies that they will be able to use throughout their school years to read and comprehend complex literary and informational texts independently and proficiently, a Common Core Standard intended to prepare students for college and career reading.

RELATED COMMON CORE STATE STANDARD

Anchor Standards for College and Career Reading
Range of Reading and Level of Text Complexity
Standard 10:

- Read and comprehend complex literary and informational texts independently and proficiently.

THE CASE

Reviewing Previously Learned Reading Strategies

The lesson began with Mr. Dunbar asking, "What is your favorite book of all time?" Alexandra responded that the Harry Potter series was her favorite because it has magic in it. Molly said she selected a different book as her favorite because "it has lots of booky things, British words like incubators, and stuff like that." After much deliberation, Harold selected *The Wind-up Bird Chronicle* (Murakami 1997) and stated, "It is the first time that a book has combined a fairy tale and action. It has funny things; it has sad things. I think it's a very good book."

Mr. Dunbar explained how he was glad that his students were enthusiastic about sharing their favorite books because it made him feel good as a teacher that his students enjoyed reading so much. He also stated, "I like listening to the different things . . . you had a couple of different genres that you liked. You liked word choice in your book and it was funny, and you had some background knowledge in the magic that you liked."

Mr. Dunbar asked, "Those of you who raised your hand and had a favorite book . . . how many of you have read that book more than once?" About twenty students raised their hands. Mr. Dunbar continued, "This is one of the things I am going to talk about for a little bit, about reading strategies, and then we're going to get specifically into a certain kind of reading strategy. You all have been very interactive with the book. You've read it numerous times; you could probably quote parts of the book. . . .

That is one of the things we've been talking about with all of the reading strategies that we've been going over. The questions, reading with a purpose, inferencing, making connections, and what we're going to talk about today with visualization is that reading needs to be interactive. You have to look at the book and do something with the book, think about the book, because if you don't, it goes away."

Using Expository Texts to Demonstrate the Importance of Interacting with a Text

Mr. Dunbar then read aloud an expository text entitled "Pandas in Peril" (Rice 1995) that he placed on the overhead projector (see appendix for text). As Mr. Dunbar read, he modeled various forms of interaction with the text. After reading the first section of the text, Mr. Dunbar asked, "How many people have ever seen a Giant Panda?" About twenty-five students raised their hands. One student said he touched a panda and Mr. Dunbar responded, "Oh, you've got to share that story. How did you get to touch a panda? Were you kicked out of the zoo, or was it on purpose?" The student shared, "It was on purpose. I just walked up, and it was right there at the edge and I reached out and touched it." Mr. Dunbar responded, "Cool! Wow! You got to touch a panda. That's very neat."

After Mr. Dunbar read aloud the next section of text, he stopped and commented on the fact that only 1,000 pandas currently live in the wild. Then he pointed out that

650 students attended their elementary school and that
more students attend their local high school then there
are pandas in the wild. A student shared, "I did a paper on
that," indicating he had written a paper on pandas. The
teacher replied, "That's right, you did the paper and I'm
going to have you share a couple of things when we get a
little further, okay?"

Mr. Dunbar read another section of the text about a
Westerner who was allowed into China to study pandas.
Mr. Dunbar once again modeled the reading strategy of
questioning. He stated, "I wonder why he was the first
one they ever let in, and in 1980." A student conjectured,
"Maybe because, like a lot of the people from America,
from the other Western countries, they hunted pandas or
something." The teacher responded, "Maybe there was a
conflict between the Chinese government, and they didn't
want to let other people in."

Mr. Dunbar read the next section of text. As he read,
the student who had written a paper on pandas interjected
with various facts and insights from his research, such as
"They [hunters] laid traps that were hidden down there to
catch them [other animals], but pandas would get caught
in them."

After the teacher concluded the read aloud, he asked,
"What did you guys find interesting about this one?" Jo-
seph commented about how stiff the penalties were for killing one panda. Another student mentioned that it was interesting that there were only 1,000 pandas left in the wild.

Mr. Dunbar then displayed another expository text
entitled "Cheetah" on the overhead. The teacher read the

text quickly and straight through, with little expression and without stopping for comments from the students or himself (see appendix for text). "Okay, if we took a test on these two, which one are you going to do better on?" Mr. Dunbar asked after reading the text. The entire class responded, "The panda one!" One student offered that even though Mr. Dunbar just read the cheetah text, "we didn't discuss it." Mr. Dunbar replied, "We didn't discuss it; I read too fast, but you guys are just being lazy because look. Look how small that print was, look how much . . . less text there is . . ." Then Mr. Dunbar explained why he read the text about cheetahs after he read the text about pandas by saying, "I read it [cheetah text] second for you so that you would remember it more. Diego?" Diego responded that the cheetah text sounded boring. Danny stated that they did not get to question the cheetah text. Mr. Dunbar asked, "Okay, how many of you have ever read like the panda paper? Your favorite book. The first time you read it, did you read it like the panda paper or the cheetah paper?" "The panda paper!" the students responded together.

Mr. Dunbar then shared that he purposely manipulated the text as a means of getting a particular response from students. He stated, "I knew Scott had known something about it, so I was talking to him about it. I had other people. We talked about the zoo. Diego had a personal connection to it, so we discussed it a little bit. All of that interaction about the text—and you all said that you would do better. . . . You have to interact with text."

Mr. Dunbar listened to more of his students' comments about and connections to the text as he retrieved several books from his desk. Then he said, "Basically the idea behind all of the reading strategies I have been going over and that we have reviewed is, you have to interact with the book. Just a simple interaction, which doesn't take a lot of work—takes you twice as long to read sometimes, maybe even longer than that—but just that simple, little interaction increases what you remember about the story and how well you remember it."

Visualizing a Narrative

After Mr. Dunbar reiterated to his students the importance of employing reading strategies and creating textual interactions to support their reading comprehension, he explained the reading strategy of visualization. Then he stated, "One of the books that I read when I'm making up my lessons made an interesting point about visualization that I want you to think about now. Creating scenes and pictures increases your level of engagement, and books become interactive. And that's what I want you to think about today."

Mr. Dunbar explained to his students that he was going to read to them a narrative text about fireflies (Brinckloe 1985/1986). He said to his students, "Think about fireflies. What connection do you have? We're not going to share them right now, but I want you to think about connections that you have. Visions that come to your mind. Images." Mr. Dunbar explained that he was going to read the text about fireflies to them after he told them a personal story about his son and the text on fireflies.

Then Mr. Dunbar explained how his son, who was too young to read, flipped through the text on fireflies. At first, his son thought the fireflies were stars. But as his son turned the pages, he was able to infer that the pictures were of fireflies and not of stars. Mr. Dunbar pointed out that although his son could not read, he was able to surmise that the text was about fireflies, based solely on visualization.

Before reading the narrative text about fireflies, Mr. Dunbar provided his students with explicit directions. He stated, "I want you to take a few minutes as I'm reading. I'm going to go nice and slow as I turn the page. I am going to purposely move slowly, and I'm not going to show you any of the pictures because I want you to draw the pictures in your mind. And then I am going to stop at a certain point and have you get into some groups, and I'm going to get you some scratch paper, and you bring your pencil over, and then I want you to sketch it out." Then Mr. Dunbar read the text on fireflies (see appendix for text).

At one point, Mr. Dunbar stopped reading and commented, "Think about that one for a little bit. My friends took jars of fireflies to different homes. I want to show you that picture." He showed the picture to his students and several of them nodded. He commented, "I saw a couple of people nodding, 'Yeah, that's what I thought.'"

Mr. Dunbar continued reading. Selecting another stopping point in the text, Mr. Dunbar said, "Now we're going to get into groups, and I'm going to read that next page, and I'm going to have you do it. I promise I'm going to continue to read." Mr. Dunbar counted off students in fours (1, 2, 3, 4) and asked them to form groups according to the appropriate numbers. Students quietly and quickly formed their groups. Once the students were settled in their groups, Mr. Dunbar read the previous page aloud a second time. Then he said, "On your paper right now, draw that image. I will read it one more time while you're working." The students individually drew their images as they listened to Mr. Dunbar reread the page.

As his students worked, Mr. Dunbar moved around the room observing what his students drew and commenting in a low voice to some of them so as not to disturb the other students. He provided positive feedback. To one student he said, "That looks nice. It looks like a combination of the fireflies around the moon, but it kind of also looks like the bees around the honeycomb, like on Winnie the Pooh; it's the same sort of visual. If it was at night you wouldn't be able to tell the difference. You know what I mean? Because you're not using color. I like that; it looks nice."

As his students worked, Mr. Dunbar informed them when they had a minute and when they had thirty seconds left to work. When time was up, Mr. Dunbar asked his students to put their pencils down and listen as he read the last page. Just as before, his students listened as he read the last page of the text aloud. Then Mr. Dunbar reread the page several times and his students sketched their drawings.

When Mr. Dunbar finished rereading the last page of the text, his students silently looked at their group members' drawings. He asked his students to comment on each other's drawings instead of commenting on their own drawings. A student noticed that the drawings had "some of the same ideas, but did not look exactly alike."

Mr. Dunbar continued, "If Mrs. Montrose [principal] walked in and saw all of your pictures, would she understand that you were all drawing about the same thing?" The students all agreed that the principal would not see the exact same drawings but would understand that the drawings were based on the same text.

Mr. Dunbar summarized, "Now, thinking about what you just did. You took more time to do this than you probably will in other circumstances. But thinking about the interaction you just had with the text: we didn't talk about questions, we didn't ask questions, we didn't answer stuff, we didn't set up prior knowledge with the book, but we visually interacted with this book, and you did something very, very visual. If somebody were to pick this book up three years from now, would you remember? Do you think you would remember at least part of this book?" The students affirmed that they would remember some of the text. Then Mr. Dunbar shared the pictures from the text. The students compared their drawings to the pictures in the text and to the drawings of the other students. Mr. Dunbar stressed that there was not a right or wrong answer, but different interpretations.

Visualizing a Poem

Mr. Dunbar then transitioned to visualizing with another type of text, poetry. Before reading the poem "Daffodils" by William Wordsworth, Mr. Dunbar reviewed some vocabulary words in the poem. He had these words listed on the overhead. After teaching these vocabulary words, Mr. Dunbar placed a copy of the poem on the overhead (see appendix for poem).

When Mr. Dunbar finished reading the poem, he asked, "How many people in their mind, images raced through? Even things as simple as 'when on my couch I lie in vacant or in pensive mood,' I just pictured myself lying on the couch . . . even that helps me interact with this [text] so that I constantly remember this poem." Then a student shared her experiences of lying on a couch. The teacher replied, "And when you are lying on the couch in a vacant or in a pensive mood, what would be nicer to think of than 10,000 daffodils blowing in the breeze?" Another student responded, "20,000!" Smiling, Mr. Dunbar conceded, "Okay, all right, thinking of 20,000! Yes." Mr. Dunbar and his students continued to share the images they pictured when they listened to the poem.

At the end of this lesson, Mr. Dunbar stated, "We talked about how interacting with the text is very, very important. You have to interact with the text if you want to remember what you read. Now remember, here is the key: You are in school. Sometimes you have to remember what you read . . . And so sometimes, by making a conscious effort to purposely use reading strategies, you will improve your comprehension and remember what you read better."

QUESTIONS

1. What did Mr. Dunbar hope to accomplish by asking students about their favorite books?

2. What are some examples of Mr. Dunbar modeling his metacognitive processes as he employed the various reading strategies? What are some other metacognitive strategies you have learned about that could be incorporated into the lesson?

3. Why did Mr. Dunbar choose to engage students in visualization twice, once with a narrative text and once with a poem?

4. What classroom management techniques did Mr. Dunbar use throughout this lesson?

APPENDIX[1]

Text 1: Pandas in Peril by Larry Rice[2]

Eat, sleep, wander through the forest when you're bored. What a great life the panda has. No school, no chores, not even many enemies. Great, huh? Wrong! The Giant Panda is in big trouble, deadly trouble.

Just Plain Cute

With Mickey Mouse ears, black and white coats and cuddly looking bodies, Giant Pandas appear sweet and comical. Most people find them just plain cute. They are shy, gentle creatures that generally avoid encounters with each other and with humans. But encounters with civilization are getting harder and harder to avoid. The Giant Panda is one of the Earth's most endangered species; only about 1,000 pandas survive in the wild.

---

1 The texts in the appendix have been taken off the audiotape and appear as read by Mr. Dunbar.

2 Reprinted here by permission of the author, Larry Rice.

What's the Problem?

The panda's plight is confusing. The animals have few natural predators; namely the leopard. People all over the world seem to love them, and the Chinese government considers the panda a national treasure. So why is the species on the brink of extinction? In 1980, George Shaller, a world-famous wildlife biologist, began researching that question. He became the first Westerner ever invited by China to study the panda in its native habitat. For four years he tracked pandas throughout the forest. What he found was disturbing. Pandas were in trouble. Hunters stalked pandas for their valuable hides, killing many each year. Many other pandas died at the hands of careless hunters who were actually after other species. Not only that, but the pandas were losing their homes. Humans cut down the trees and plowed the soil in their quest for wood and land.

A Brighter Future? Maybe

The Chinese government and international conservation groups are working to ensure the panda's survival. Because of their efforts, the panda's become an international symbol of conservation, but no one knows whether the results will be triumph or tragedy. Here's how humans are trying to save the panda.

Tougher Laws

Killing pandas is illegal in China, but until 1987 the penalty was not severe; only two years or less in prison. Now people who kill pandas or try to sell the animals' fur face life in prison, sometimes even death!

New Safer Homes

Many new panda reserves have been created and there are plans to designate almost all of the animal's range as protected zones. Tree cutting will be restricted or banned. People living in reserves will move elsewhere when possible.

More Panda Pathways

New forests are being planted to link panda regions. This will provide food and cover for the animals as they travel between their territories. It will not be easy, but there is still hope that one of the planet's most adorable creatures can be saved.

Text 2: Cheetah

Physical Characteristics: Head and body length is 1.1 to 1.5 meters (4–5 feet); tail length 600–800 millimeters (24–32 inches); shoulder height is 700–900 millimeters (28–35 inches); weight is 35–72 kilograms (75–160 lbs.). Cheetah paws are very narrow compared to those of other cats and their claws are blunt and slightly curved and only partly retractable.

Habitat: Semi-desert through open grassland to thick brush.

Habits: Cheetahs are mostly active during the day; they can climb and often play in the trees. They are the fastest terrestrial animals. Maximum speed ranges from 50–75 mph, but maximum speed can only be sustained for a few hundred yards. Their diet consists of gazelles and impalas, the calves of large ungulates and sometimes small mammals and birds. In captivity, cheetah diets include ground meat mixtures, chicken fryers and vitamin and mineral supplements.

Social Habits: Cheetahs occur alone or in small groups consisting of a female with cubs or 2 to 4 related males. Cheetahs make a variety of sounds including aggressive vocalization, purrs of contentment, a chirping sound made by a female to her cubs, and an explosive yelp.

Reproduction: Wild female cheetahs normally give birth at intervals of 17–20 months. The gestation period is 90–105 days. There are usually three to five cubs per litter. Cubs weigh 5–10 ounces at birth. They open their eyes after 4–11 days and are weaned when they are 3 to 6 months old. The cubs are taught by their mother how to hunt. They separate from her at the age of 15–17 months and attain sexual maturity at 21–22 months. Captive cheetahs have lived up to 19 years; in the wild the lifespan is 10–12 years.

At the Philadelphia zoo, the first cheetah at the zoo arrived in 1879. Since then we have had a total of 29 cheetahs. Improvements in nutrition and animal management at our zoo contributed to the world's first captive cheetah births in 1956. Today we participate in the cheetah species survival plan and are working with colleagues in Zimbabwe to rescue, breed, and study cheetahs in the wild.

Conservation: The cheetah is an endangered species because of excessive hunting of both cheetahs and their prey, the spread of people and their livestock into cheetah habitat and the fur market. To learn more about how you can protect cheetahs in their natural habitat, you can write to ONE WITH NATURE, c/o Philadelphia Zoo, 3400 West Girard Avenue, Philadelphia, PA 19104.

Text 3: Fireflies by Julie Brinckloe[3]

On a summer evening, I looked up from dinner, through the open window to the back yard. It was growing dark. My tree house was a black shape in the tree and I wouldn't go up there now. But something flickered there a moment. I looked, and it was gone. It flickered again over near the fence. Fireflies.

"Don't let your dinner get cold," said Momma. I forked the meat and the corn and potatoes into my mouth.

"Please, may I go out? The fireflies!" Momma sighed and Daddy nodded.

"Go ahead," they said. I ran from the table down to the cellar to find a jar. I knew where to look, behind the stairs. The jars were dusty and I polished one on my clean shirt, then I ran back two steps at a time. Holes, I remembered, so they could breathe. And as quietly as I could—so she wouldn't catch me dulling them—I poked holes in the jar with Momma's scissors. The screen door banged behind me as I ran from the house. If someone said, "Don't!" I wasn't listening.

I called to my friends on the street: "Fireflies!" But they had come before me with polished jars, and others were coming behind. The sky was darker now. My ears rang with crickets and my eyes stung from staring too long. I blinked hard as I watched them. Fireflies. Blinking on, blinking off. Dipping low, soaring high above my

---

3 Reprinted here by permission of the author, Julie Brinckloe.

head, making light patterns in the dark. We ran like crazy, barefoot in the grass.

"Catch them, catch them!" we cried, grasping at the lights.

Suddenly a voice called out above the others, "I caught one!" and it was my own. I thrust my hand into the jar and spread it open.

The jar glowed like moonlight and I held it in my hands. I felt a tremble of joy and shouted, "I can catch hundreds!" Then we dashed about, waving our hands in the air like nets, catching two, ten, hundreds of fireflies, thrusting them into jars, waving our hands at more.

Then someone called from my house, "It's time to come in now!" And the others called from other houses and it was over. My friends took jars of fireflies to different houses.

I climbed the stairs to my room and set the jar on a table by my bed. My mom kissed me and turned out the light.

"I caught hundreds," I said.

Daddy called from the hallway: "See you later, alligator!"

"After a while, crocodile," I called back. I caught hundreds of fireflies. In the dark, I watched the fireflies from my bed. They blinked off and on, and the jar glowed like moonlight, but it was not the same. The fireflies beat their wings against the glass and fell to the bottom and lay there. The light in the jar turned yellow like a flashlight left on too long. I tried to swallow, but something in my throat would not go down. And the light grew dimmer, green, like moonlight underwater. I shut my eyes tight and put the pillow over my head. They were my fireflies! I caught them. They made moonlight in my jar, but the jar was nearly dark. I flung off the covers, I went to the window, opened the jar, and aimed it at the stars.

"Fly!" Fireflies, blinking on, blinking off. Dipping low, soaring high above my head, making circles around the moon, like stars dancing. I held the jar, dark and empty, in my hands. The moonlight and the fireflies swam in my tears. And I could feel myself smiling.

Text 4: Daffodils by William Wordsworth

I wandered lonely as a cloud that floats high over vales and hills
When all at once I saw a crowd, a host of golden daffodils.
Beside the lake beneath the trees, fluttering and dancing in the breeze.
Continuous as the stars that shine and twinkle on the Milky Way
They stretched in never-ended line along the margin of the Bay.
Ten thousand saw I at a glance, tossing their heads in a sprightly dance.
The waves beside them dance, but they outdid the sparkling waves in glee
A poet could not be but gay in such jocund company.
I gazed and gazed but little thought what wealth to show me,
What wealth the show to me had brought.
For oft when on my couch I lie, in vacant or in pensive mood
They flash upon that inward eye, which is the bliss of solitude.
And then my heart with pleasure fills, and dances with the daffodils.

Commentary on Case 6: A Teacher Educator's Perspective

Rose Marie Codling

> "You have to look at the book and do something with the book, think about the book because if you don't . . . it goes away."
>
> (Mr. Dunbar)

In a lesson on visualization, what a perfect mental image Mr. Dunbar's remarks create. I imagine watching the smoke from an extinguished match disperse and disappear within a few seconds' time. I believe this image will resonate with any reader who has had difficulty concentrating during reading, trouble recalling what was read, or simply failing to get the main idea. Who hasn't had the experience of reading something only to think back, unable to understand or remember? Sometimes, it just "goes away."

An important objective of this lesson appears to be introducing, modeling, and giving students an opportunity to practice making mental images during reading. Mr. Dunbar accomplishes this well in ways that will be discussed below. More impressive in this lesson, however, is how the teacher approaches the instruction in a way that is sure to enhance students' selective and independent application of strategies. In short, the lesson facilitates metacognition at every turn.

The lesson begins as many typical lessons do. The teacher engages students in a discussion that is based on something with which they are familiar. Mr. Dunbar uses students' personal reading to generate interest in the lesson. In this particular lesson, however, this approach serves another purpose. Talking about the high level of engagement in their personal reading helps the students to conceptualize what it means to *interact with text*, an important theme that is repeatedly reinforced throughout the lesson.

Early in the lesson, Mr. Dunbar mentions four reading strategies that have previously been taught and indicates to the students that they will add a fifth strategy to their repertoire. They will learn about visualization, another strategy that will accomplish the goal of increasing their interaction with text. As the lesson gets under way, Mr. Dunbar reads to students and engages them in lively discussion by asking questions, commenting on interesting points in the reading, enthusiastically responding to students' comments, and guiding them to make personal connections to the reading. He variously reviews previously taught strategies by defining or modeling them. He draws students' attention to their own strategy use as they question the text, make personal connections, or make inferences. Each of Mr. Dunbar's actions (activating prior knowledge, encouraging personal connections, guided discussion, reviewing previously taught strategies) facilitates his objective by preparing the students for the introduction and application of the strategy of visualization.

Excellent strategy instruction conveys three kinds of information to students (Paris, Lipson, and Wixson 1983) and each kind of information is evident in Mr. Dunbar's lesson. Commonly referred to as declarative, procedural, and conditional, these types of knowledge each make an important and unique contribution to successful strategy instruction (Pressley, El-Dinary, Gaskins, Schuder, Bergman, Almasi, and Brown 1992). Declarative knowledge includes factual information about the strategy and its structure.

- Mr. Dunbar explained to his students that he was going to read to them a narrative text about fireflies. He said to his students, "Think about fireflies. What connection do you have? We're not going to share them right now, but I want you to think about connections that you have. Visions that come to your mind. Images."
- He asked his students to comment on each other's drawings instead of commenting on their own drawings. A student noticed that the drawings had "some of the same ideas, but did not look exactly alike." Mr. Dunbar continued, "If Mrs. Montrose [principal] walked in and saw all of your pictures, would she understand that you were all drawing about the same thing?" The students all agreed that the principal would not see the exact same drawings but would understand that the drawings were based on the same text.

Procedural knowledge enables the reader to engage in the steps of the strategy. Effective strategy instruction conveys the procedure to students so that they can independently apply the strategy to their reading. Almasi

(2003) found that this was the most difficult aspect of strategy instruction for teachers. Indeed, this appears to be the case with Mr. Dunbar as well. In one example, Mr. Dunbar nicely modeled self-questioning during discussion.

- Mr. Dunbar read another section of the text about a Westerner who was allowed into China to study pandas. Mr. Dunbar once again modeled the reading strategy of questioning. He stated, "I wonder why he was the first one they ever let in, and in 1980."

More often, however, he "hints" at how to conduct the strategy, but he stops short of explicitly modeling for students how to do it themselves.

- "I am going to purposely move slowly, and I'm not going to show you any of the pictures because I want you to draw the pictures in your mind. And then I am going to stop at a certain point and have you get into some groups, and I'm going to get you some scratch paper, and you bring your pencil over, and then I want you to sketch it out."
- Then he said, "On your paper right now, draw that image. I will read it one more time while you're working." The students individually drew their images as they listened to Mr. Dunbar reread the page.

Conditional knowledge commonly answers three questions—*Why do I need to learn this strategy? How will it help me? When is it appropriate to use it?* Knowing how the strategy will help and when to use it are critical questions asked by a metacognitive reader. A metacognitive reader is a thinking reader. When readers are metacognitively aware, they constantly analyze tasks and texts, select appropriate strategies, and monitor their understanding and their own strategy use as they read.

What is most impressive in this lesson is the way Mr. Dunbar integrates conditional information throughout the entire lesson. Constant reminders are important to reinforce with students why the strategy is important and how it will help them. There are numerous examples of Mr. Dunbar's conveyance of conditional information in this lesson.

- "That is one of the things we've been talking about with all of the reading strategies that we've been going over. The questions, reading with a purpose, inferencing, making connections, and what we're going to talk about today with visualization is that reading needs to be interactive. You have to look at the book and do something with the book, think about the book, because if you don't, it goes away."
- Mr. Dunbar then shared that he purposely manipulated the text as a means of getting a particular response from students. He stated, "I knew Scott had known something about it, so I was talking to him about it. I had other people. We talked about the zoo. Diego had a personal connection to it, so we discussed it a little bit. All of that interaction about the text—and you all said that you would do better. . . . You have to interact with text."

- Then he stated, "One of the books that I read when I'm making up my lessons made an interesting point about visualization that I want you to think about now. Creating scenes and pictures increases your level of engagement, and books become interactive. And that's what I want you to think about today."

- Mr. Dunbar summarized, "Now, thinking about what you just did. You took more time to do this than you probably will in other circumstances. But thinking about the interaction you just had with the text: we didn't talk about questions, we didn't ask questions, we didn't answer stuff, we didn't set up prior knowledge with the book, but we visually interacted with this book, and you did something very, very visual. If somebody were to pick this book up three years from now, would you remember? Do you think you would remember at least part of this book?" The students affirmed that they would remember some of the text.

- "By making a conscious effort to purposely use reading strategies, you will improve your comprehension and remember what you read better."

Overall, there are many positive features in Mr. Dunbar's lesson. The students are engaged and the teacher's actions are carefully planned to achieve his instructional objective. Mr. Dunbar provides important declarative and conditional information throughout the lesson. More explicit modeling of procedural information using think-alouds would further strengthen this nicely designed lesson.

Commentary on Case 6: An English for Speakers of Other Languages (ESOL) Perspective

Rebecca L. Oxford

To me Mr. Dunbar's reading lesson was striking because he effectively merged his pedagogical topic—strategies for reading comprehension and recall—with several content themes over different genres. He led the children in using strategies to interact with the panda story. One of the most dramatic pedagogical devices emerged when Mr. Dunbar read aloud the cheetah story with no children interacting with the text after having just held a detailed, personalized discussion of the panda story. Mr. Dunbar asked the children which of the two, the panda story with interaction and the cheetah story with no interaction, would help them do better on a test. The children chose the panda story and explained that they discussed it. The teacher used this as a teaching tool to emphasize the importance of interacting with the text, and the students got the message clearly.

Mr. Dunbar also taught two types of visualization strategies: making mental images and drawing pictures. This was a very good move, as the students could relate to both. Because of visualization, the children found it easy to deal with an image-rich poem by Wordsworth.

At the same time he also helped students personalize the material (e.g., by asking questions, such as "What is your favorite book of all time?" "How many of you have read your favorite book more than once?" and "How many have seen a Giant Panda?"), by comparing the number of remaining pandas in the world with the number of students in the children's school and in the local high school, and by adding his own personal story about his son "reading" a storybook through pictures alone.

It is very difficult to do all this in one lesson and keep the lesson coherent, yet Mr. Dunbar managed to do this quite deftly. His knowledge of students' needs, interests, and background certainly helped with this. Since this class was a "diverse" group these different comprehension strategies are particularly important. Differences in strategy use, as well as in reading proficiency, are often related to specific linguistic and cultural backgrounds (see Oxford 1996; Oxford, Cho, Leung, and Kim 2004). Teachers need to note and be responsive to the linguistic or cultural differences in their class.

Case 7

Coordinating and Employing Multiple Strategies to Comprehend a Science Fiction Text

Fifth-Grade Reading Lesson

CASE SETTING

This reading lesson was taught by Leslie Gabriel, a veteran teacher of thirty-five years, at Brookfield Elementary School on May 16. The reading/language arts block took place from 9:30 to 11:00 in a heterogeneous classroom setting. During this block, Gabriel taught three small reading groups. Ms. Gabriel met with this particular reading group from approximately 10:15 to 10:40. This group consisted of nine students who were reading on grade level. At the beginning of the year, most of these students had been reading on a third grade level. Many of these students were born in countries other than the United States, and English was their second language.

CASE OVERVIEW

This case illustrates small group reading instruction where students were taught to coordinate and employ multiple reading strategies (Brown, Pressley, Van Meter, and Schuder 1996), including visualizing, making connections, summarizing, and predicting, to comprehend a science fiction text (National Reading Panel 2000). Ms. Gabriel explained and modeled these multiple reading strategies (Duffy, Roehler, Sivan, Rackliffe, Book, Meloth et al. 1987). She selected a science fiction text entitled *The Green Book* (Walsh 1982) for her students to read and introduced them to the characteristics of the science fiction genre. This case illustrates ways in which Ms. Gabriel developed her students' metacognitive thinking skills (Paris, Cross, and Lipson 1984), their use of multiple reading strategies (NRP 2000; Pressley and Wharton-McDonald 2006), and their knowledge of the science fiction genre (Goldman and Rakestraw 2000). Throughout this case, students quoted accurately from a text to explain what the text said explicitly and to draw inferences. They came to the discussion prepared and drew on their preparation as well as their own knowledge to participate in the discussion. These two features of the case illustrate two of the Common Core Standards.

RELATED COMMON CORE STATE STANDARD

Grades 4–5
Reading Literature
Standard 1:

- Quote accurately from a text when explaining what the text says explicitly and when drawing inferences from the text.

Listening and Speaking
Standard 1:

- Come to discussions prepared, having read or studied required material.
- Explicitly draw on that preparation and other information known about the topic to explore ideas under discussion.

THE CASE

Ms. Gabriel began class by overviewing the day's reading assignments with the whole class. She had work for three reading groups listed on the board. This group was reading *The Green Book* (Walsh 1982), a science fiction text about families' exodus from a dying Earth to a new planet, which the children help save. Ms. Gabriel expected the other students in the class to work independently at their seats while she taught this small reading group.

Ms. Gabriel called the group to a large table in the back of the classroom with their completed comprehension questions. The students had read one or two chapters in *The Green Book* at the time of this lesson. On a chalkboard next to the table, she had written the following question: "What might the settlers look for on the new planet to solve their needs?" Underneath the question, Ms. Gabriel made three columns and wrote the following headings at the top of each column: *Survival Needs, Personal Needs*, and *Emotional Needs*.

Using the Strategy of Identifying the Characteristics of a Story's Genre

Ms. Gabriel began the lesson with an instructional conversation about genre. "First of all, let's talk about, this book is very different than some of the books that we've read. In fact, it's definitely a fiction book. What kind of fiction does this tell about? When we think about the book that we just read, *She Wanted to Read* (Carruth 1966), that book told a story about someone, and it was real. And if we also look at the book that we read before that, *The Cabin Faced West* (Fritz 1987), did that talk about something also? Was that a real thing that we could think about and picture? What's different about this book? Angela?" Angela stated that the book wasn't real. Ms. Gabriel asked, "What do you mean it's not real?" Angela clarified, "It hasn't happened." Ms. Gabriel said, "It probably hasn't happened, certainly not that we know about. So it's something that could happen when?" Some students responded, "Later on in the future." Ms. Gabriel continued, "Later on in the future. What do you call that, Saul?" Saul responded,

"Science fiction." Ms. Gabriel responded, "Excellent, Saul. We call it science fiction. So is this book going to be hard for us to visualize and relate it to something we know?" "Yeah," Saul admitted. Ms. Gabriel confirmed his response and stated, "So we're going to have to use our imagination. We're going to have to use maybe other books we've read, or maybe other movies that we saw, so that when you think about what's happening, we can visualize it more."

Using the Strategy of Reviewing the Story's Setting, Characters, and Plot

Ms. Gabriel and her students reviewed the first chapter's setting, characters, and plot. The students talked about the setting in the first chapter. Sabrina said the setting was on a spaceship, and they determined that the time frame must be in the future. Ms. Gabriel also asked her students to identify the events that occurred in the first chapter and list them in chronological order. The students stated that the characters had to leave planet Earth, and that the characters gathered survival supplies to take with them. These supplies included an ax, two pairs of clothes, food, and a saw. The students said that the characters left Earth on a spaceship and traveled for four years.

Using the Strategies of Visualizing, Summarizing, and Predicting

After Ms. Gabriel's students reviewed the setting, characters, and plot of the first chapter, Ms. Gabriel facilitated an instructional conversation to help her students make connections and visualize. After mentioning that the characters were in the spaceship for four years, Ms. Gabriel said, "So right away we're like going, oh, imagine being in a car for four years." "No way," Daniel responded. Ms. Gabriel encouraged her students to imagine that scenario and asked if there was anything else that they questioned. Angela expressed concern that the characters could only bring two pairs of clothes. Sergio suggested that their clothes might not fit them after four years. Ms. Gabriel said, "You think in four years, that's good. You know what? I never thought of that. Their clothes might not have fit them after four years. Okay."

Ms. Gabriel and her students continued their instructional conversation about what happened in the rest of the chapter. All the students paid attention and participated. This conversation led them to make predictions about what might happen when the spaceship landed. Ms. Gabriel stated, "Okay, we're going to talk about that kind of stuff in a few minutes because we're going to predict, we're going to think about the new planet and some of the problems that they might have or some of the things they're going to look for when they find a new home." As the instructional conversation continued, Ms. Gabriel asked her students to summarize some of the problems in the first chapter. The students determined that the characters would need to find someplace to live.

Using the Strategy of Answering Questions

Next, Ms. Gabriel had her students share their responses to the comprehension questions and items they had answered prior to meeting as a group. Ms. Gabriel asked Sabrina to read the first item. Sabrina read, "People in *The Green Book* are leaving the planet Earth for a reason

that is not given. Predict what you think the reason is."
Ms. Gabriel asked, "Did we get some idea when we read
what the reason might be?" Sabrina responded, "Yeah."
Ms. Gabriel responded, "All right. What does the word
predict mean? If it says predict, what does that mean?"
Daniel answered that it means "what you think will happen." Ms. Gabriel responded, "What you think based on
what? Based on your background knowledge."

Then Ms Gabriel asked Saul to read another item.
Saul read, "Explain the fear the children had about the
journey." Ms. Gabriel responded, "How many of you
have ever taken a trip and been afraid, had fears about
the trip? I know I have." Saul said he did too. Then Ms.
Gabriel made a connection to a personal experience. She
said, "The first time I was in a plane, I was in the plane,
and before I left I wrote a letter to my sons and told them
how much I loved them, you know. Of course, I didn't
write to my husband because he was with me, but because
I thought if the plane crashed I wanted them to get it, so
what might be a fear that you might have on a trip?" Jacob
said, "That something bad could happen."

Connecting an Unfamiliar Situation to What Students Know

When Ms. Gabriel and her students finished reviewing
the comprehension items, they turned their attention to
the graphic organizer on the board. This graphic organizer
contained three columns, each with one of the following
headings: *Survival Needs*, *Personal Needs*, and *Emotional
Needs*. Ms. Gabriel initiated an instructional conversation
on these three types of needs.

Ms. Gabriel began by addressing survival needs. She asked Angela to give her a survival need, something that the children would need when they reached the planet. Angela replied, "They're going to need water." Ms. Gabriel prompted her students to identify other survival needs. Daniel responded, "A house." Ms. Gabriel said, "I'm going to use a different word. What's the word I should use instead of a house?" Daniel said, "Shelter." Ms. Gabriel responded, "Shelter, because finding a house might be more difficult for them. Something else?" Saul said, "Food." Ms. Gabriel wondered if they would find a place that had food already.

When a student, Mamta, suggested that they would need medicine, the instructional conversation shifted to personal needs. Ms. Gabriel responded, "You're saying medicine. Do you think that's a survival need? I mean, do you think they'll find this on the planet? Should we list that under survival need or maybe under personal need?" Mamta decided that medicine was a personal need.

Then Kyle suggested the children would need clothes. However, he did not identify clothes as a personal or survival need. Ms. Gabriel asked, "Where do you want me to put that? Personal or survival? Where do you want me to put it?" Kyle responded, "Survival." Ms. Gabriel said, "Okay, because certainly clothes are kind of like protection, especially if it snows, if it's cold."

Ms. Gabriel directed the instructional conversation back to personal needs. She said, "Okay. All right. Personal needs. Think about it. You're going on the ride. Here we are in the spacecraft. Okay. What do you want to find, or what is going to be important to you? What do you need personally to be able to survive on this place? Person-ally. Think about the personal things that you like about your life. Sabrina?" Sabrina said, "Probably something to play with." "All right, things to play with, should I put?" asked Ms. Gabriel. Ms. Gabriel turned to the group and asked for other personal needs. Several students said, "Electricity." Ms. Gabriel confirmed that electricity would be needed and pushed for her students to be honest in their responses. This prompted Kyle to shout, "TV," and Natashia to offer, "Some shopping centers." Ms. Gabriel asked, "Do we think any of these things will be there? We don't know."

Ms. Gabriel then asked the group for emotional needs. Jacob offered, "Family." Ms. Gabriel replied, "Family. Very good." Ann responded, "Friends." The students seemed reluctant to talk about emotional needs. To prompt them, Ms. Gabriel asked, "Something else?" When Sabrina of-fered, "Going to school," Ms. Gabriel responded, "Is that an emotional need? Is that a personal need? Not really. It doesn't—either one of those, it doesn't really fit in. It might be something you enjoy doing, but it really isn't an emotional need." Ms. Gabriel prompted the students further by asking, "What makes you happy?" This ques-tion did not spark any answers. Watching the clock and students' waning interest, Ms. Gabriel decided to bring closure to the conversation rather than clarify emotional need.

To conclude the instructional conversation about survival, personal, and emotional needs, Ms. Gabriel said, "Okay. We're going to have to think about what these kids are going to find when they get there. How many of you think they're going to find everything they need when they get there? What will they have to do if they don't find everything they need?" Sabrina said, "Make them." Ms. Gabriel responded, "Yes, they're going to have to figure out a way to get it." Ms. Gabriel gave her students an assignment and dismissed them to their seats.

QUESTIONS

1. What exactly does Ms. Gabriel do to help her students learn to use multiple strategies?
2. Ms. Gabriel teaches her students the characteristics of a genre. How would this instruction help their comprehension?
3. Ms. Gabriel had her students complete graphic organizers. How did the completion of these graphic organizers support their comprehension?
4. If time and student engagement had allowed, how could Ms. Gabriel have helped her students understand emotional needs and why "going to school" is not an emotional need? Why would this be important?

Case 8
Preparing Students to Comprehend and Learn from an Expository Text

Fifth-Grade Reading Lesson

CASE SETTING

Gayle Peterson, a fifth year teacher at Cherry Hill Elementary School, taught this lesson one morning in late May. The class met in a portable, with the room arranged in three long horizontal rows, each of which contained seven desks. The class consisted of a heterogeneous mix of students: half were Hispanic, about 25 percent African American, and 25 percent White. One student was of Asian heritage. Almost two-thirds of this group were or had been in FARMs, and most of the Hispanic students were or had been in ESOL classes. Two students had, or once had, IEPs. During this ninety-minute lesson, Ms. Peterson met with her students in two small reading groups that she formed on the basis of reading level. The first group, comprising struggling readers, had seven students; the second group had eight. The lesson for both groups focused on preparing to comprehend and learn from a social studies text and lasted about thirty-five minutes each. Both lessons integrated literacy instruction and social studies instruction (Morrow et al. 2002).

CASE OVERVIEW

In this reading lesson, Ms. Peterson prepared two groups of students to read an expository text entitled *If You Lived at the Time of the American Revolution* (Moore 1998). First, she introduced them to three questions that they would eventually be answering as they read the text: Why did the author include these details? Who would find the information useful? and What is one thing someone can learn about this topic? To prepare them to answer these questions, Ms. Peterson worked with her students to identify and record information on KWL charts (Ogle 1986). A KWL chart contains three columns of information: What I Know, What I Want to Know, and What I Learned. Ms. Peterson's goal for both groups had been to complete the first two columns on the KWL chart, read a short section of text, and after reading answer the question, *What is one thing someone can learn about this topic?* Both groups of students filled in the first two columns by reviewing what they already knew about the American Revolution and previewing text features (NRP 2000). The first group was unable to read the text and answer the question in the time allotted for their group. Ms. Peterson altered the pacing of the second group so that they could read a small excerpt from the expository text and answer the question. In this case, students used text features to locate information and preview an expository text, addressing a Grade 3 Common Core Standard. Whereas the Standard is Grade 3, the students are using a book appropriate to their study of the American Revolution, a common curriculum goal for fifth grade social studies in many states.

RELATED COMMON CORE STATE STANDARD

Grade 3
Reading Informational Text
Standard 5:

- Use text features and search tools (e.g., key words, sidebars, hyperlinks) to locate information relevant to a given topic efficiently.

THE CASE

Ms. Peterson expected her students to work independently at their desks while she conducted small group instruction. She began the lesson by explaining their independent work to her students. After her students began their independent work, Ms. Peterson called the first small group of students to meet with her.

Teaching a Group of Struggling Readers Strategies for Comprehending Expository Social Studies Text

Ms. Peterson distributed to each student in the group the expository text *If You Lived at the Time of the American Revolution* (Moore 1998) and a KWL chart. Then she asked her students to write the topic *American Revolution* on the top of their KWL charts while she wrote it on a small whiteboard.

Ms. Peterson directed her students' attention to a piece of chart paper on which she had written the three questions. *Why did the author include these details? Who would find the information useful? What is one thing someone can learn about this topic?* Ms. Peterson continued, "Pay special attention to this one [pointing to the third question] because this is going to be an exit card."

When Ms. Peterson finished presenting the exit card question, she directed her students' attention to their KWL charts. To complete the *What I Know* column of their KWL charts, Ms. Peterson asked her students to "take about three minutes to think of everything you know about this topic." Students responded that they didn't think they knew anything. As students began to work on the first column, Ms. Peterson reassured them, "Just think back to during social studies. I'm sure you know something. You'll be surprised how much you already know. The American Revolution. Do you know what it was? Think about the words. *American*. So therefore it has to deal with what country?" A student responded, "America." Ms. Peterson continued, "Revolution. Revolt. What does *revolution* mean? What does *revolt* mean? See if you can make some connections." The students continued to add information to the *What I Know* column of their KWL charts.

After three minutes, Ms. Peterson invited her students to share their responses. Artem said, "It was a war in America." Enrique said, "It has something to do with the Act." Ms. Peterson inquired, "Which Act?" One student answered, "The Quartering Act." Another student offered, "The Tea Act?" Ms. Peterson said, "See, I told you guys you already knew a lot!"

Once students had shared their responses, Ms. Peterson directed their attention to the *What I Want to Know* column in their KWL charts. She asked, "What do you want to know about the American Revolution?" She informed them that they had three minutes to "list at least five things." After three minutes, Ms. Peterson invited her students to share their responses in question format. She also said to them, "If there's a question that's not on your list, you want to put it down." Students volunteered, "When did it happen? What year?" "Why did it happen?" "Who made it happen?" Ms. Peterson said, "Take your thinking a little further. Besides 'Who made it happen?' what about 'Who took part in the American Revolution?'" Other students offered, "Why was it important?" "Who won?" "Who fought in the war?" "Where was the war?" "Where can we find information about the American Revolution?" Ms. Peterson wrote students' questions on the whiteboard. After students had shared all of their questions, Ms. Peterson explained that they would answer these questions in the *What Have I Learned* column after they found all of their resources.

Pointing to *If You Lived at the Time of the American Revolution*, Ms. Peterson said, "I am giving you a resource. Tell me, what type of text is this? Is this fiction or nonfiction?" Several students responded, "Nonfiction." Ms. Peterson continued, "And how do you know? Raise your hand. How do you know this is nonfiction?" Julie answered, "Because the American Revolution was real." Ms. Peterson affirmed her response and continued, "Another thing, it's a textbook. Okay. And part of our objective is to read for information using textbooks."

Next, Ms. Peterson asked her students to preview the text by looking at the text features to determine if they could use this book to answer the questions in the *What I Want to Know* column of their KWL charts. After a few minutes, Ms. Peterson asked, "What did you look at to preview your book? What text features did you look at? Enrique?" Enrique replied, "The table of contents." Ms. Peterson continued, "All right. What information did you find from the table of contents?" Enrique reread the table of contents and offered a chapter title called, "What Started the Revolution?" Ms. Peterson affirmed his response.

To guide the discussion, Ms. Peterson asked, "What other text features can you use to preview the book?" Anita responded, "Picture," referring to the picture on the front cover of the text. Ms. Peterson responded, "The picture. Yes. What do you think this is a picture of?" Anita replied, "Of the American Revolution." Ms. Peterson continued, "Let's say if we were to divide this picture in half. There are some people on this side and this side. What do you notice about the folks on this side of the book?" Anita responded, "They're happy." Ms. Peterson said, "And laughing. Which, think back to social studies, when we were talking about how the group separated into, how the colonies were separated into about three groups. Which group do you think these people belong to?" Several students responded that those pictured were colonists. Ms. Peterson explained that they were all colonists and reminded her students that the colonists were divided into various groups. The students identified two of the groups, the Patriots and Loyalists. Then Ms. Peterson asked, "Why do you say they were Loyalists?" Kainda replied, "Because they are sad." Julie said, "They look like they're all rich and handsome. And the kid is holding a British flag." Ms. Peterson concluded the discussion about the picture by explaining, "So these are some of the textual features you want to look at when you're reading for information, or like when you're trying to find a resource as to whether or not this is going to help me answer my questions."

Ms. Peterson then directed her students' attention back to the table of contents. She pointed out to them that the author wrote the chapter titles in the table of contents in question format. Then she read aloud the student-generated questions that she had written on the whiteboard, ending with the question, *Where can I find information about the American Revolution?* "Well, we already know the answer to this last question," she noted. "In this book," a student explained. Then Ms. Peterson instructed her students to open their texts to the table of contents. She said, "Put a little dot next to the chapters you think we should read in order to answer these questions. Okay? Take about three minutes. You're looking at your table of contents."

After three minutes, Ms. Peterson asked, "What were some of the chapters you identified that can be useful to help us find our answers?" Anita suggested the chapter title "What Started the Revolution?" Kainda suggested the chapter title "What Ended the War?" Ms. Peterson agreed with both of these chapters and instructed her students to put dots next to their titles. Next, Ms. Peterson asked Marco to share. Marco offered the chapter title "Did Any Women or Children Fight in the Continental Army?" Ms. Peterson asked, "That question is going to help us answer which question?" Marco replied, "Who fought in the war?" A fourth student suggested the chapter title, "What Was Life Like before the Revolution?" Ms. Peterson answered, "Yes. What question will this chapter help us answer?" The student replied, "Why did it happen?" and Ms. Peterson agreed. A fifth student suggested, "What Words and Expressions Came from Life during the American Revolution?" Another student disagreed that this chapter would be helpful. Ms. Peterson explained, "Remember, we're not reading the entire book. We just want to focus on chapters that will help us answer our questions."

The time was almost up for this first group, so Ms. Peterson instructed students to answer a revised exit card question. She reminded students, "Even though our topic is on the American Revolution, we really didn't read anything as yet. However, we went through the text to see, okay, is this useful information?" She explained that their exit card question would be somewhat different: *What is one thing someone can learn about previewing a nonfiction text?* She added that they were to write the exit card question on the back of their KWL charts and answer it when they returned to their seats. Then Ms. Peterson dismissed the group.

Altering the Pace of Instruction for a Group of Students Reading on Grade Level

Ms. Peterson called the second group to meet with her. She began by focusing her students' attention on the same three questions that she had presented to the first group of students: "*Why did the author include these details? Who could find this information useful?* and last but not least, *What is one thing that someone can learn about this topic?* You're going to be using the last question as an exit card. So as we're going through today's lesson, make sure you are paying attention to the last question." Then Ms. Peterson handed out KWL charts. She asked her students to write their name, the date, and the topic, *American Revolution*, on the top of their charts.

When the students completed writing the heading on their KWL charts, Ms. Peterson asked them to complete the *What I Know* column. She said, "What I want you to do now, and you guys can do it independently, and we're going to move faster, is come up with at least five things that you think you know about the American Revolution." As students worked, she reminded them, "Think of topics we've discussed in social studies. Look at the title. What can you tell from the title?" A student answered, "It's a war." "That's something you know! Write it down," she explained. A short time later, another student asked, "Did it give us independence?" "Write it down. Write it down," Ms. Peterson urged. Then she asked, "Where did it take place? France? Spain? England?" "Here!" a student responded. As Ms. Peterson's students recorded information in the *What I Know* column of their KWL charts, she urged them, "If you think you know it, write it down."

After a few minutes, Ms. Peterson invited her students to share their responses. Femi asked, "Wasn't King George the leader?" Ms. Peterson responded, "Okay." Another student offered, "It took place in America." Ms. Peterson replied, "All right." A third student said, "It's a war." Ms. Peterson repeated this response, and then said, "All right. Good." Another student added, "It took place in England." Then Ms. Peterson said, "Now remember, this whole section is what we think we know. We may be wrong. We may be correct. We'll find out."

Once students had shared their responses, Ms. Peterson directed their attention to the *What I Want to Know* column in their KWL charts. She asked, "What do you want to know about the American Revolution?" Then she explained that they had three minutes to think of and record at least five things that they want to know. She reminded them to write these five things in question format.

After allowing three minutes for this task, Ms. Peterson said, "Look through your list. You have five. Some of you have more than five. Think about the most important thing that you have written down that you'd like to learn about." Students shared their questions. "When did it happen?" "What were the results of the American Revolution?" "What was the Revolutionary War about?" "Where did it take place?" "Were taxes involved?" "Who was included?" "How did it start?" When another student offered, "Who started it?" Ms. Peterson responded, "Good question. Just like with a fight. We want to know whose fault it was. Right? Who started the fight? Who pushed first?" As the students shared their questions, Ms. Peterson wrote them on the whiteboard. She reminded her students to write down any questions from the whiteboard that they had not written on their KWL charts. She explained that they would answer these questions later when they got to the *What I Learned* column of their KWL charts.

Then Ms. Peterson distributed to each student in the group the expository text, *If You Lived at the Time of the American Revolution*. She said, "We're going to be using this nonfiction text to see if this text is going to help us answer these questions. Let's take a quick minute, a quick minute, to preview." She continued, "Can this book help us address all of these topics?" As the students previewed the text, Ms. Peterson prompted them to use text features other than the pictures. Then she asked, "Which specific textual feature or textual aid can help us definitely determine if this book is something we should read?" Paki responded, "The table of contents." Ms. Peterson replied, "The table of contents. Yes." As the students examined the table of contents, Femi and Terry noted that the author had written the chapter titles in question format.

After discussing the table of contents, Ms. Peterson asked Jason to read aloud the student-generated questions on the whiteboard. Jason read the questions. Next, Ms. Peterson said, "We have to answer these questions because these are the questions you guys want to learn more about." Then she instructed her students to put a dot next to the chapter titles in the table of contents that they think might answer their questions. She said, "You're looking at the table of contents to see which chapters we should read in order to answer these questions. Okay. You have a minute and fifty-two seconds."

After approximately two minutes, Ms. Peterson asked Kelly, "Which chapters do you think we should read?" Kelly identified the chapter "What Started the Revolution?" Femi suggested the chapter "What Ended the War?" And Jason offered "Did Everyone in the Colonies Take Sides?"

Ms. Peterson replied, "Take sides? Which question is that going to address?" "Who were in it?" Jason answered. Then Ms. Peterson read the chapter title, "What Was Life Like before the Revolution?" "Which question would that address?" she asked. Students answered, "What was the Revolutionary War about?" "When did the American Revolution take place?" Ms. Peterson responded, "Yeah. Okay. What was going on before the war? What about the chapter, 'Did Any Women or Children Fight in the Continental Army?' Which one do you think that could answer?" A student responded, "Who were involved in it?" "Yes. Yes. Okay? So you want to make sure you're looking carefully at your resources before deciding if this is a credible book or not," Ms. Peterson explained.

Following this discussion, Ms. Peterson instructed her students to read the first chapter in the text and answer the exit card question. She said, "You're going to read starting on page 12 on your own, because we only have about seven minutes left. All right? So quickly read page 12, and be ready to answer the exit card, based on the information on page 12 and 13. It's a short chapter. 'What Was Life Like before the Revolution?'" After her students read for a few minutes, Ms. Peterson reminded them to answer the exit card question on the back of their KWL charts. She said, "*What is one thing someone can learn about this topic*? You just read 'What Was Life Like before the Revolution?' So write one thing someone can learn about this topic and give support." Ms. Peterson informed her students of the time remaining to read the chapter and answer the exit card question. She said, "You guys have about three minutes left to do that." When the timer went off, Ms. Peterson dismissed the group.

QUESTIONS

1. Ms. Peterson used the KWL chart to help students access their background knowledge before reading. What exactly did she do? How would her instruction enhance both students' understanding of the text and their learning in social studies?

2. Ms. Peterson used the KWL chart to help students preview the text before reading. What exactly did she do? How would her instruction enhance students' understanding of the text and their learning in social studies?

3. Ms. Peterson introduced three questions that students would be answering as they read: *Why did the author include these details? Who would find the information useful?* and *What is one thing someone can learn about this topic?* How would answering these questions enhance students' understanding of the text and their learning in social studies?

4. Ms. Peterson altered her pacing so that the second group would be able to complete all of the tasks that she had planned. What exactly did she do to alter the pacing? What do you think the trade-offs might have been?

II
PERSPECTIVES
ON TEACHING:
COMMENTARIES

A Matter of Principle:
Evidence of Learner-Centered
Psychological Practices among
Effective Teachers

Patricia A. Alexander

The cases offered in this enlightening volume came from the work of teachers who participated in the High-Quality Teaching Project. When the High-Quality Teaching Project was first conceptualized, researchers contemplated various theoretical frameworks that might serve in the design and implementation of this important undertaking (Valli and Croninger 2001). Certainly the literature was replete with discussions of exceptional or master teachers and of pedagogical practices deemed to be appropriate for all students or for those identified with special needs, such as children raised in a culture of poverty (Kilpatrick, Swafford, and Findell 2001). One of the frameworks that proved useful to us, especially in the development of assessment measures was the learner-centered psychological principles (LCPs) (American Psychological Association [APA] Board of Educational Affairs 1995; LCP Work Group of the APA Board of Educational Affairs 1997). Those principles, which arose from extended discussions among renowned psychological researchers, were founded on more than a century of educational philosophy and empirical research within five broad areas: development and individual differences; the knowledge base; strategic processing or executive functioning; motivation and affect; and situation or context.

For the purpose of this commentary, I return to those five areas of research to consider what lessons about learner-centered psychological principles can be derived from select teaching cases presented in this volume. Specifically, I want to talk about general patterns that I observed across these illustrative cases and use the choices and activities of just one teacher to highlight those patterns: Leslie Gabriel (Cases 3, 5, 7), who offers guidance through her interactions with her fifth graders about various literacy topics, including vocabulary development and comprehension strategies.[1]

My reason for returning to LCPs is to explore the degree to which these principles derived from theory and research remain viable when put into the context of the classroom and placed in the hands of a competent teacher like Ms. Gabriel who is operating within the challenging

---

1 See companion volume, *Upper Elementary Math Lessons: Case Studies of Real Teaching*, for a comparable analysis of mathematics lessons.

and dynamic context that is today's classroom. What aspects of the principles were consistently and more readily apparent in the practices of this highly effective teacher, and which principles were less evident? Further, what explanations can be forwarded for those principles that are strongly espoused in the literature but not often seen in the day-to-day activities of this select teacher?

DEVELOPMENT AND INDIVIDUAL DIFFERENCES

> Learning, although ultimately a unique adventure for all, progresses through various common stages of development influenced by both inherited and experiential/environmental factors. (Alexander and Murphy 1998, 36)

One of the most intriguing patterns that emerged across these cases was the seeming contrast in Ms. Gabriel's thoughtful attention to the developmental levels of students as a whole, but the more limited consideration of individual students' unique strengths or needs. It was quite evident that Ms. Gabriel was aware of and responsive to the developmental level of her students. As we look into her classroom, we see a teacher who has chosen reading activities that she feels are well matched to the ages, capabilities, life experiences, and overall interests of her students. In addition, Ms. Gabriel is vigilant for signs that she has either chosen well or missed her instructional mark, and she is ready to make whatever adjustments seem appropriate.

For instance, Ms. Gabriel seemed aware that her students would need support if they were going to demonstrate understanding of such comprehension skills as predicting. For that reason, she took time to remind them of what it means to predict and prompted them to engage in prediction with a familiar situation (i.e., personal trip) before that comprehension strategy was practiced in a more novel context (i.e., space flight).

Unless teachers like Leslie Gabriel are attuned to the developmental level of their students, they cannot hope to guide those children toward optimal academic development. However, effective teaching and learning also requires educators to pay attention to students' *unique* cognitive, motivational, sociocultural, and physical attributes; that is, their individual differences. We see some trace of this attention to individual differences when Ms. Gabriel instigated discussion of her students' particular quirks in conjunction with their writing of their own autobiographies following the reading of the autobiography *The Lost Garden* (Yep 1996). So, as a model for the class, Ms. Gabriel shared what she sees as certain students' quirks, such as Omar's outspokenness and his extensive background knowledge.

What we do not see, however, is how such knowledge and awareness of students' individual differences translate into the individualization of curricular materials and activities. Generally speaking, the teachers in these reading cases appear to deal with student diversity through the use of small instructional groups who work on similar or collaborative learning activities. Why would that be the case? Why would teachers as competent as Ms. Gabriel not demonstrate greater sensitivity to students' individual strengths and needs through lesson modifications or personalized tasks? The simplest explanation might be that teachers do not have the time or the freedom to modify instruction to match the uniqueness of an entire class of students. Three groups working on three varied tasks may be the most variability teachers can manage without classrooms becoming overly complex or chaotic. As an alternative, teachers may be able to introduce individual and independent activities for students that are sprinkled into the curriculum. Ms. Gabriel's autobiography activity, for instance, allows students to bring their own personalities and interests to the foreground even as the class works collectively on the instructional goals.

THE KNOWLEDGE BASE

One's existing knowledge serves as the foundation of all future learning by guiding organization and representations, by serving as a basis of association with new information, and by coloring and filtering all new experiences.

(Alexander and Murphy 1998, 28)

If there has been one learner-centered psychological principle that has found its way into the routine practices of competent teachers, it relates to the tremendous influence that students' prior knowledge and experiences exert on their subsequent learning. In many of the cases in this volume, teachers took care to activate their students' existing knowledge relative to the topic or skill under consideration. Often through initial questioning or through some form of small group activity, the capable educators represented in these cases sought to draw out and build on what their students already understood or their existing facilities.

As a strategic educator, Ms. Gabriel was especially careful to bring her students' existing knowledge and experiences to the foreground when she anticipated that the ensuing concept or task would be especially abstract, novel, or challenging. Ms. Gabriel was quite adept at using verbal exchanges—what the case writers referred to as instructional conversations—to uncover what her students thought or had experienced when she was targeting their vocabulary knowledge. Her thoughtful questions as well as her feedback and elaborations were powerful tools in her pedagogical repertoire.

Moreover, when the conversations during Ms. Gabriel's literacy lessons were combined with some prior reflections and reviews, the outcomes were especially informative. For example, before joining their reading group to discuss the vocabulary in *Justin and Best Biscuits in the World* (Walter 1986), students had worked independently on their vocabulary webs—graphic tools that required them to locate the sentence in the story; write a definition, synonyms, antonyms; and generate their own sentence with the target word. Through this exercise, Ms. Gabriel had ensured that students came to their small group with some exposure to the target words. When the conversation with the first small group ensued, Ms. Gabriel soon became aware that several of her students had focused on lexically similar words—*strange* for *strained* and *retarded* for *retorted*. In this case, students' world knowledge was somewhat of a barrier to their subsequent learning.

If I have a particular concern with what I discerned in these chosen cases, it was that the approaches these reading teachers use to activate students' knowledge base occasionally have the appearance of well-practiced techniques or classroom routines. While such routines are necessary elements within a highly functional classroom (Shulman 1987), they may have the secondary effect of lessening the depth of reflection in which students engage. Consider the vocabulary web that Ms. Gabriel used when introducing new words from the story. Such a graphic resource is very useful and is clearly better than the old "look it up and use it in a sentence" approach my teachers used in teaching new words. However, if this web were used every time that target words were presented in Ms. Gabriel's classroom, then the pedagogical potency of such a useful technique could be abated. Consequently, teachers would be advised to use various knowledge activation techniques and to use them in a flexible manner—just enough novelty or creativity to keep students on their toes.

MOTIVATION AND AFFECT

> Motivational or affective factors, such as intrinsic motivation, attributions for learning, and personal goals, along with the motivational characteristics of learning tasks, play a significant role in the learning process.
>
> (Alexander and Murphy 1998, 33)

Young or novice learners require learning environments that pique their interests and energize them. But they also need help to set the seeds for deeper and more durable forms of motivation that will promote their academic development. As these cases make apparent, highly capable teachers like Ms. Gabriel have the ability to establish a caring and motivating learning environment (Mitchell 1993). Through her choice of activities, interaction styles, and general concern for her students, Ms. Gabriel has established learning communities that encourage participation. For example, even though Ms. Gabriel did not shy away from correcting students' misunderstandings or directing them toward more conventional meanings or procedures, she did so in a nonjudgmental way.

We see this when Ms. Gabriel recognized that her students' efforts to categorize particular needs as survival, personal, or emotional were less than optimal. When Mamta suggested that medicine should be slotted under survival needs during discussion of *The Green Book* (Walsh 1982), Ms. Gabriel subtly questioned Mamta's choice. Through Ms. Gabriel's feedback and self-reflection, she led Mamta and the others to reconsider her categorization approach. In effect, by being supportive while calling upon students to rethink and justify, Ms. Gabriel navigated the difficult boundary between critiquing and caring.

Although Ms. Gabriel and the other effective teachers in these reading cases are quite proficient in orchestrating engaging and motivating learning environments, they are seemingly less invested in planting the seeds of individual interest in students. This relates to our earlier discussion of individual differences. What would make these classrooms even more learner-centered would be evidence that teachers were incorporating the particular interests and experiences of each and every student into the activities within the learning community. Allowing for some degree of student choice and self-determination can be one step toward fostering students' individual interests.

We can speculate for a moment on why there was more collective than individual attention to students' motivational as well as cognitive needs in these classrooms. Perhaps the simplest explanations relate to factors of time and organization. That is, it takes a great deal of planning and implementation time to individualize instruction, to say nothing about the information that teachers would require about each student to make that happen. Further, curricular organization in the form of lessons, activities, and resources is more geared to whole class or small group instruction as we observed throughout these cases. Consequently, it would fall to the teachers to modify existing curricula to address these personal characteristics. For whatever reasons, one-to-one interactions between teacher and student remain rare occurrences.

STRATEGIC PROCESSING AND
EXECUTIVE FUNCTIONING

The ability to reflect on and regulate one's thoughts and behaviors is essential to learning and development.

(Alexander and Murphy 1998, 31)

In her lesson on the science fiction book, *The Green Book* (Walsh 1982), Ms. Gabriel recognized the importance that her students' metacognitive and comprehension reading strategies play in their literacy development. Thus, those strategies became the centerpiece of that lesson. But what

Ms. Gabriel also demonstrated by her actions was awareness that students, even those performing at or above grade level, need support and even explicit instruction in how to operate strategically. For that reason, Ms. Gabriel not only prompted her students to predict during discussion of *The Green Book*, but she took time to have them explain what prediction meant and to lead them through some helpful examples.

As we witnessed in these cases, however, even an experienced teacher like Ms. Gabriel may be more inclined to *mention* the need for strategic behavior than she is to directly and expressly teach students how to engage in strategic learning. Thankfully, there is a resurgence of interest in the teaching of strategic processing, which may well translate into more explicit teaching of critical cognitive and metacognitive procedures (Alexander, Graham, and Harris 1998). Although I applaud this newfound interest in strategic processing and executive functioning, I and others (Afflerbach, Pearson, and Paris 2008) remain concerned that important distinctions between skills and strategies, which are both essential for development in any academic domain, are being confused and muddled by researchers and practitioners alike. Thus, while the use of strategies (i.e., effortful, reflective, and non-routine processes) are mentioned in school curricula, it appears that skills (i.e., automatic, habitual processes) are actually the goal.

SITUATION OR CONTEXT

Learning is as much a socially shared understanding as it is an individually constructed enterprise.

(Alexander and Murphy 1998, 39)

Learning never occurs in a vacuum. It is always influenced by the time and place, and by the individuals who populate the classroom environment. Throughout these informative reading cases, we observed teachers who were very sensitive to the socially shared nature of learning. Whether they were interacting with the entire class or working with small groups of students, Ms. Gabriel and the other effective reading teachers often took advantage of the social nature of learning. These educators seemed to recognize that they did not have to be the sole sources of information or feedback in their classrooms and they appreciated that there were alternative perspectives and approaches to learning and performance that needed to be shared. Nonetheless, Ms. Gabriel and these other teachers remained the quiet authorities within their classrooms and ensured that this community of learners functioned effectively and efficiently.

Another feature of these cases that pertains to this principle was the manner in which Ms. Gabriel thoughtfully constructed activities that made the learning process more concrete and hands-on for her students. Whether it was Ms. Gabriel's graphic summaries or a teacher's visualization activities, these highly capable teachers understood that abstract concepts or complex procedures would be better grasped and communicated when situated in more familiar settings with more concrete objects and behaviors. Even their simple acts of inviting students to participate verbally or physically in the whole class or small group activities were additional evidence that these educators were skilled at harnessing the power of the situation and context to facilitate their students' learning.

If there is a question regarding this particular learner-centered principle, it is the issue of transfer. While concrete, hands-on, and highly familiar activities are effective tools in the acquisition of concepts and procedures in literacy, the dependency on such tools should wane over time, as should students' dependency on either human or nonhuman resources in the learning environment. Ideally, the concepts and procedures learned well in one context or situation should, in effect, migrate or transfer to other relevant situations. In this way, students' knowledge, strategies, and skills become broader and deeper and do not remain tentative or context-reliant. For example, we would hope that Ms. Gabriel's students could contemplate the meaning of words without the aid of a vocabulary web.

CONCLUDING THOUGHTS

Throughout this volume, I have had the pleasure of encountering a number of teachers who have dedicated themselves to the academic development of their students. Moreover, these educators have embodied much of the knowledge and processes described in the learner-centered psychological principles and the vast literature upon which those principles were based. We can be encouraged that there are educators like Ms. Gabriel who face the challenges and complexities that are inherent within the educational system with such competence and professionalism. As educational researchers, we benefit from the lessons these educators provide us, just as their students benefit daily.

Moral Dimensions on Teaching Reading

Daria Buese

The word "moral" is one that causes uneasy feelings in some people, especially when used in the same sentence as "teaching." For these individuals, the idea that teaching is a moral endeavor inspires visions of children being led to a specified belief or value system. Indeed, when we talk about morals we *are* talking about what is valued by society at large, and the thought of teachers addressing moral values in school simply makes some people uncomfortable. One inevitable question: "Whose morals are we talking about?" nearly always arises when conversations about education turn to the idea that teaching and moral values are intertwined, and may be the very question that pops into your mind as you read this commentary. Teachers, whether or not they speak about their teaching in moral terms, display moral values (for better or for worse) every day in their work with their students. In this commentary I examine the moral dimensions of teaching (for better) in the practice of two of the teachers whose lessons are presented in this book. I begin by presenting a short introduction to what I mean by the moral dimensions of teaching and examine ideas of other scholars on the subject. It is my intent in writing this commentary that you will be given fuel for thought on the moral aspects of your own teaching because the very act of teaching sends moral messages to students in virtually everything teachers do in their classrooms. Teachers can either be cognizant of this condition of their work or deny it, but I steadfastly believe that recognizing it gives us a way to analyze and improve our practice. As moral agents we help make schools into places where children can flourish socially and intellectually. Rather than shying away from conversations about the moral dimensions of our teaching for fear of controversy, such discussions should be encouraged for their potential to advance commonly shared educational values.

MORAL DIMENSIONS

The literature around the moral dimensions of teaching encompasses a wide range of issues including broad societal concerns about the purposes of schooling. As important and interesting as these issues are, they can also confound discussions about what is moral in teaching practice, so I will not address the larger moral landscape of teachers' work here. Rather, I am more concerned about the moral meaning in the day-to-day work teachers do with their students. Teachers cannot avoid sending moral messages to students and it is in accepting this fact of school life that they can begin to notice how the way they interact with students and the instructional decisions they make convey moral meaning. David Hansen (2001) portrays this idea eloquently and provocatively by stating: "Teaching is a moral endeavor because it influences directly the quality of the present educational moment" (831).

Consider what the present educational moment might entail as you think about the moral dimensions of teaching—I offer a few suggestions. Teachers send moral messages to students through their choices of instructional materials and how they present intellectual ideas (Fenstermacher, Osguthorpe, and Sanger 2009; Jackson 1986; Tom 1984; Valli 1990). By choosing reading texts, for example, that portray characters as people who are subject to the consequences of their decisions and actions, teachers introduce moral dilemmas into the classroom. Through discussing the moral decisions the characters make with students, teachers blend the intellectual task of teaching reading with the investigation of such positive moral values as fairness, kindness, and truthfulness in the face of uncertainty and injustice. Teachers model moral values of respect and care through the way they talk to their students and listen to their ideas. When teachers consistently call for similar behavior in their students and when they instill the virtues of learning and teaching that Starratt (2005) identifies as presence (connection to the content being studied), authenticity (truthfulness to self or being "real"), and responsibility (understanding learning as a value and willingly participating in it), they help students recognize and practice behaviors that contribute to learning for all of their students. By getting to know their students, what they like, dislike, the things they care about, their lives outside of school, and so on, teachers develop responsive, reciprocal relationships with their students that help students feel cared for (Noddings 1984). When students feel cared for and cared about, they are more willing to take intellectual risks, which, even when modest, can advance their understanding of academic concepts.

Fenstermacher (2001) helps us understand the moral in teaching by describing what he terms the "manner in teaching." This is a method in which teachers instill moral and intellectual values in students.[1] He explains that manner in teaching is what teachers do to convey virtuous conduct. With attention to the contentiousness of certain words, he reminds us that some people would argue that a teacher's "manner" could include conduct that is good and/or bad. In his research about the moral manner in teaching he states that his interest is in understanding the manner in teaching that "picks out what is good, moral, sound, and defensible about persons, rather than what is bad, immoral, silly or stupid about them" (649). It is in this vein that I highlight some of the moral dimensions of teaching that appear in this book.

When the researchers (myself included) who collected the data that resulted in this book set out to understand the practices of reading teachers, we were more interested in their teaching of content than the moral dimensions of their teaching. However, as I have noted, teaching is

---

1 See the *Journal of Curriculum Studies, 33*(6) for articles produced by the Manner in Teaching Project, directed by Gary Fenstermacher and Virginia Richardson. The articles in this journal provide insight into what is morally salient in teachers' day-to-day work. The authors also investigate the moral grounding of schools and classrooms and provide clear images and discussion of how teachers nurture the moral development of their students.

imbued with moral meaning, so even in the short excerpts of lessons presented here, we can see how the teachers conveyed virtuous conduct and created learning environments that supported their students' intellectual and moral development. I could easily pick out the moral dimensions of teaching in any of the lessons featured in this book; however, I present only two. I do this in an effort to be succinct, but also because moral messages are often very subtly sent—they may be conveyed through tone of voice, a look, or a nod. Therefore, I've selected two examples that are more overt and in doing so hope to make "moral" and "teaching" more compatible concepts for those who do not (yet) view them as such.

MR. DILORETTO (CASE 4)

I begin with Mr. DiLoretto's fifth grade reading lesson. The lesson demonstrates how the combination of text choice and instructional conversations around moral issues contributes to students' reading comprehension as well as their moral development (Clare and Gallimore 1996). The lesson opens with Mr. DiLoretto engaging his students in a discussion of the book *The Borning Room*. Although the students were reading other books in their smaller literature discussion groups, he chose this one to read aloud to the students. This choice represents an instructional decision that blends the intellectual with the moral. Granted, the academic objective of the lesson was an exploration of character traits, but consider the many moral dimensions of this choice of text. Mr. DiLoretto noted that some of the students talked to him about the book outside of class.

They told him it seemed like a "dark book," indicating that it provoked thinking about ideas that were disturbing to them. The book is about serious issues—marriage, birth, death—but weaves upsetting scenarios with joyful ones. Using *The Borning Room* provided Mr. DiLoretto with an opportunity to learn about his students' emotional responses to life events in a fictional context. It provided an avenue for his students to solicit discussions with him about moral issues outside of class. They clearly felt cared for by their teacher; he was someone to whom they could safely voice their thoughts and they trusted him to respond to their ideas without fear of having their thoughts discounted as immature or irrelevant. As the in-class discussion of *The Borning Room* unfolded, it was apparent that Mr. DiLoretto had created a classroom climate over time in which students were unafraid to talk about their feelings and experiences about complex issues that have no clear answers. Moreover, the discussion we see in the lesson shows that the classroom climate encouraged open disagreement with others' viewpoints as long as participants' perspectives could be justified and articulated.

In another instance in the same class, a small group of students discussed whether Rose, a character in the book *The Root Cellar*, is selfish or polite. Mr. DiLoretto prodded a student, Bai, who had been silent up to that point to give his opinion. Bai complicated the discussion by commenting, very eloquently, that Rose acted as she did because "she feels lonely in her heart. . . . Like she just wants to go home and she doesn't really know where her home is." Mr. DiLoretto immediately "showcased" (Fenstermacher 2001) Bai's response by asking him to repeat what he said. Showcasing allowed Bai to be acknowledged for the quality of his response. In this way the student's thinking, rather than the teacher's, became an example of a thoughtful, intellectually concise response. This episode demonstrates another aspect of Mr. DiLoretto's moral manner in teaching. By showcasing Bai's idea, the teacher encouraged others to develop their own moral perspectives and sent all his students the message that the ability for moral reasoning belongs not only to adults, but children as well.

MS. HINTON (CASE 2)

Ms. Hinton's fourth grade poetry lesson shows moral dimensions of teaching that are a little less overt than Mr. DiLoretto's, but it offers a particularly good example of a method for fostering moral conduct that Fenstermacher (2001) describes as characteristic of moral manner in teaching. He refers to this particular method, one he found in the teachers he researched, as the "design and execution of academic task-structures." Through her modeling of poetry reading, Ms. Hinton explicated the kind of academic performance (an intellectual virtue) she wished for her students to attain.

Precise exposition of academic performance was particularly important in Ms. Hinton's case given the students in her class. Twenty-five percent of Ms. Hinton's students received ESOL services and almost half were Hispanic. In the school district in which this lesson took place, students who were identified as ESOL students were simply those who were the least proficient in English. Many immigrant students and children of immigrants lost their ESOL designation before reaching fluency in English and received all of their instruction in the regular classroom. Ms. Hinton's moral agency with these English language learners appeared through the precision with which she communicated her expectations for student performance in preparing a poetry reading for the class. She modeled reading poetry and discussed how punctuation works to convey an image. She stressed her belief that poetry is an artistic medium that is enhanced through the readers' audible interpretation of it.

These may not be unusually difficult ideas to discuss in a typical fourth grade language arts lesson, but consider how difficult these concepts might be for English language learners and how challenging it would be for any fourth grader to perform poetry reading publicly, in front of his or her peers. Ms. Hinton's demonstrations, the ensuing discussion, and her suggestions for practicing their readings set the stage for students to be successful in accomplishing a public performance of poetry reading with the additional goal of gaining an understanding about the nature of poetry. An aspect of the lesson that I found particularly significant to the moral aspects of teaching was that the students did not make light of Ms. Hinton's performance nor did they object to the prospect of performing for the class themselves the next day. The teacher's expectations for decorum can be surmised by what the students did not say or do during the teacher's presentation. Consider how this class might look without Ms. Hinton's attention to the academic task structure. Do you think students would be more or less motivated to practice their reading of poetry in a serious way if the teacher had simply made the assignment without carefully modeling and defining her vision of a high-quality performance?

I add one more detail about Ms. Hinton's lesson that reveals a moral dimension of her teaching. Many teachers of immigrant children comment that the students' parents are unable to help their children with homework because they don't speak English well enough or are not familiar with American educational routines. Ms. Hinton helped the students come up with ways to practice their poems, either alone, in front of a mirror, or in front of someone in their family. There are at least two important moral dimensions in this practice. First, she let her students know that there was no excuse for not practicing their presentations even if there was no one at home to practice with. The moral message was clear; there was no positive virtue in coming to class unprepared. Additionally, she also provided the students with a unique opportunity to obtain parental help with their homework. The assignment did not require the parents to understand the content of the homework or even the academic value of the assignment. The nature of the assignment did, however, create an opportunity for parents to talk to their children about what they were doing in school. Thus, Ms. Hinton's second moral message to her students was that she desired and appreciated parental participation in schoolwork and expected her students to solicit it. In doing so she created a bridge for parents to increase their involvement in their child's learning of school subjects.

MORE FUEL FOR THOUGHT

I had the privilege to observe some of the lessons that were presented in this book and talk to the teachers about their teaching. As you might expect, their attention to the moral dimensions of teaching was much richer in the real life of their classrooms than these lesson excerpts reveal. However, I maintain that my ability to characterize "the moral" in their practices, despite the abbreviated versions of their lessons as they are presented here, confirms how morally saturated the act of teaching is. The examples of the moral dimensions of teaching I commented on may seem on the surface to be commonplace. You might conclude that the teachers were simply teaching in ways that are reasonably expected or that moral virtues related to intellectual growth are a natural result of teaching certain content. You may wonder, "Did the teachers really think about their practice in moral ways?" I assert, with certainty, that these teachers did approach the moral dimensions of their practice on a conscious level to promote highly valued intellectual and behavioral traits. They constructed their lessons in ways that disposed students to habits of mind that contributed to their intellectual development. They created classroom atmospheres in which students received respect from others and learned the value of returning it. And they developed caring relationships with their students in ways that helped students realize that positive behaviors and attitudes reap greater rewards than negative ones. The moral values these teachers expressed appeared purposefully, not unconsciously, within the "present educational moments" of their lessons because they understood and accepted that moral agency is implicit in the practice of teaching.

Accessing the General Education Curriculum: Ideas for Including Students with Disabilities

Deborah L. Speece, Sara J. Hines, and Caroline Y. Walker

With the reauthorization of the Elementary and Secondary Education Act in 2002 (No Child Left Behind), all students must show adequate yearly progress in reading and mathematics. The Individuals with Disabilities Education Act (IDEA) requires that students with disabilities be educated in the "least restrictive environment" possible. This means that now more than ever classroom teachers must find ways to ensure that all students grasp what is being taught. In reading instruction, teachers need techniques that will ensure that all students sufficiently master decoding, develop fluency, and comprehend what they read.

Special challenges exist when teaching reading to intermediate students, particularly those in the fourth through sixth grades. It is at this age that students transition from learning to read to reading to learn (Chall 1983). During this transition period, a teacher is likely to encounter students displaying a wide variety of reading problems (Leach, Scarborough, and Rescorla 2003). Students who had previously struggled with decoding may still be struggling to read individual words. Some students who had been average readers might begin to fall behind as more difficult reading tasks demand greater fluency and automaticity. Still other students who had never previously shown problems might begin to show difficulties in reading comprehension, due either to underlying problems in comprehension or because they struggle to integrate the processing demands of word reading and extracting meaning from text. With students showing such a wide variety of reading strengths and weaknesses, it is important that teachers be equipped with instructional strategies that meet the needs of diverse learners.

Kameenui and Carnine (1998) identified six major features of effective instruction that would serve the learning needs of most learners and would be especially important for children with diverse learning needs (e.g., children at risk of academic failure, English learners, children with disabilities) in general education classrooms. These six features are Big Ideas, Judicious Review, Strategic Integration, Primed Background Knowledge, Conspicuous Strategies, and Mediated Scaffolding. We found that the latter three were most pertinent to the language arts lessons taught by Ms. Gabriel (Case 3), Mr. Dunbar (Case 6), and Ms. Peterson (Case 8) and will use them to discuss themes across these lessons.

The first feature, *Primed Background Knowledge*, identifies the importance of teachers helping children connect what they already know to what they are about to learn. Just as seeds will not germinate in non-fertile soil, knowledge is difficult to absorb without a frame of reference. *Conspicuous Strategies* refers to the importance of making our thought processes visible to the learner. Kameenui and Carnine note that there is an important balance to be struck between having children discover strategies on their own and providing explicit instruction on strategic steps. On the one hand, "discovery" may lead to great frustration for some learners in that they never learn the shortcuts that knowledgeable people use to make learning easier. On the other hand, "explicit instruction" may lead to rote application of strategic steps and lack of understanding on how to generalize the strategies and use them flexibly. *Mediated Scaffolding* is probably the most difficult instructional tool for teachers to master. It requires providing support or a scaffold to assist learners as they progress from acquiring new skills and strategies to demonstrating independent mastery. A good example is teaching a child how to tie shoelaces. Initially, the parent provides hints or prompts ("make a bunny ear with one lace") and probably a cardboard template of a shoe so the child has a better angle to attack the problem. Gradually these aids are removed as the child demonstrates mastery with individual steps and can then orchestrate them into the finished product.

PRIMED BACKGROUND KNOWLEDGE

Kameenui and Carnine (1998) stress the importance of teachers priming background knowledge to better enable students with disabilities to gain access to the regular classroom curriculum. This emphasis on activating background knowledge is particularly important for students with reading disabilities as they (a) generally have less background knowledge than good readers because, for example, they read less, and (b) often do not apply their existing background knowledge to their reading (Gersten, Fuchs, Williams, and Baker 2001).

Ms. Peterson uses the KWL strategy to prepare her students to read the passage on the Revolutionary War. According to Ogle (1986), KWL is a three-step procedure that assists students in activating their background knowledge (What I **K**now), in setting the stage for learning (What I **W**ant to Find Out), and in consolidating that knowledge (What I **L**earned). Ms. Peterson's choice of the KWL strategy is appropriate for students with reading disabilities because it specifically addresses both of the problems likely to be encountered by students with learning disabilities (availability and application) regarding background knowledge. By asking students what they already know, all students in the class share their schema about a topic, which activates and builds their prior knowledge before reading the expository text.

At the initial stage of the strategy (i.e., "K"), teachers also can correct misconceptions. Ms. Peterson does not use the strategy in this way; however, she wisely instructs her students to check the accuracy of their background knowledge as they read the passage. Another possible step during the K section of the strategy is the categorization of student background knowledge. In this step, after students share their background information, they are asked to examine their pooled information and classify it into categories. If necessary, the teacher suggests a category and the students choose items that fit into the category. Ms. Peterson could consider including this step in her instruction.

Mr. Dunbar in his visualization lesson also impresses upon his students the importance of accessing and connecting information to background knowledge. He selects a passage on pandas because he knows that one student has preexisting knowledge about pandas. During the lesson he uses that student as an example of how a reader connects background knowledge to text. Mr. Dunbar also discusses the importance of accessing background knowledge, stating, "You need to take a minute to try to see if you can figure out what's going on by using your background knowledge."

Ms. Gabriel also shows an understanding of the importance of background knowledge in her vocabulary lesson. The words she selects for instruction are words that the students had identified as being unfamiliar in meaning or outside their frame of reference. She then helps the students learn the meaning of the unfamiliar words by relating them to the students' background knowledge. For example, she initially relates the word *scattered* to students on the school playground and then guides a student to use the word in relation to her own clothes being scattered around her bedroom. Ms. Gabriel also relates the meaning of the word *bonus* to the students' background knowledge by using it in relation to bonus questions on a test, an experience familiar to the students.

The acquisition and activation of background knowledge is particularly difficult for students with disabilities. All three of the teachers use and build the background knowledge of their students to improve their comprehension of text, therefore helping the students with learning problems in their classrooms succeed in accessing the regular education curriculum.

CONSPICUOUS STRATEGIES

Ms. Peterson introduces, models, and thereby makes conspicuous two strategies known to help students with reading disabilities and other struggling readers access the general education curriculum: text structure and KWL described above. According to Williams (2003), direct instruction that provides knowledge about text structure and explains how to use that knowledge is an effective way to improve comprehension for students with learning and reading problems. Readers who understand an author's expository organizational pattern or text structure recall more from reading texts. This skill is likely automatic for accomplished readers. Poor or struggling readers are less likely to know that they *should* examine text for its structure and less likely to know what the various structures are and how they can be useful in understanding text or recalling information. Thus, teachers need to point out text structure to such struggling readers. Peterson does this by focusing the students' attention on the table of contents, which provides an overview of the author's organizational structure, and then relating the features to the KWL framework.

Similarly, Ms. Gabriel makes use of a vocabulary web as a means of fostering deeper understanding of word meanings. The web depicts not only the standard dictionary definition but also requires students to develop their own sentence and to provide synonyms and antonyms. This framework conveys to students, visually, that understanding a word has many facets beyond the dictionary. Ms. Gabriel works diligently to help her students understand the words they selected. Her students demonstrate many problems common to poor readers. For example, Gina confuses *strained* with *strange*. In addition to helping the children come to grips with the meaning of *strained*, Ms. Gabriel could have capitalized on Gina's phonological confusion by writing both words on the whiteboard and pointing out the spelling and phoneme differences. Another instructional suggestion relates to the difficulty the children had with the nuanced meaning of *rescue*. These children may have benefited from more direct explanation. This is a case where "discovery" may have wasted too much instructional time and required a more explicit route from the teacher.

Mr. Dunbar teaches visualization as one strategy to aid comprehension. His class comprised good readers so we can only speculate on how beneficial his approach would be with children with comprehension problems. He carefully introduces the concept, reviews other strategies that the children know, and models his thinking. The visualization strategy is made concrete by having children draw their interpretation of a text that he reads aloud and then comparing the drawings. This technique may be useful for poorer readers as it makes salient the point that readers have different interpretations when they interact with text. Another positive aspect is that Mr. Dunbar reads the various passages out loud to the children. This approach would assist poorer readers in focusing on the comprehension lesson rather than struggling with decoding text that likely is too difficult for them. Mr. Dunbar understands that demonstration and modeling are important ways to help children "see" the concepts he is teaching.

MEDIATED SCAFFOLDING

Coyne, Kameenui, and Simmons (2001) identify three types of scaffolds to embed in reading instruction. One means of supporting student learning is to begin instruction with easy tasks and then move to more difficult tasks. A second approach is to build lessons around a manageable amount of information and to purposefully separate concepts that might be potentially confusing. This approach focuses student attention on discrete concepts or skills to minimize student confusion. The last scaffolding technique is to carefully move instruction from being teacher-directed to student-directed. At first, teachers should model skills repeatedly and provide many and varied examples of the concept or strategy being taught. Over time, students are given more time to work independently with less explicit modeling from the teacher. In this way, responsibility for learning is transitioned to the students themselves until they have successfully internalized the subject matter. In the lessons of Mr. Dunbar, Ms. Gabriel, and Ms. Peterson, we see examples of all three of these scaffolding techniques.

In his lesson on visualization, Mr. Dunbar engages his students with easy and personally engaging tasks before introducing new concepts and asking his students to try out a new technique for interacting with text. He begins his lesson by asking his students to share their favorite books, which they are very happy to do. From this lively discussion, he transitions to a brief recounting of reading strategies that they have already learned, setting the stage for the new strategy they will encounter in this lesson. Mr. Dunbar next illustrates different levels of reading engagement, contrasting a high level of interaction with the panda text and a low level with the story about cheetahs. The illustration begins with students simply listening to and responding to the texts; but progresses to a self-reflexive discussion of why the students preferred, understood, and remembered the panda text better than the cheetah paper. Only after he has reminded his students of the importance of reading engagement does Mr. Dunbar introduce the new reading strategy. With this new strategy, Mr. Dunbar again has his students first engage in easy tasks (simple visualization and drawing of the firefly story) before moving to a more challenging application of the lesson (visualization and discussion of the Wordsworth daffodil poem). By carefully manipulating the progression of his lesson from easier to more difficult tasks, Mr. Dunbar is able to successfully introduce a new reading strategy.

Ms. Gabriel does a wonderful job building her vocabulary lesson around a manageable amount of information.

Working with students with disabilities and English language learners, Ms. Gabriel appropriately chooses to focus her lessons on a small number of words. By keeping her focus tight, Ms. Gabriel is able to spend time guiding her students on how to decipher the meaning of the vocabulary. She is able to walk her students through reading the words in context, visualizing the context, intuiting the meaning of the word, and checking the meaning by using the word in a novel context. Ms. Gabriel also chooses words that are easily distinguished from one another, whose structure and meanings are not easily confused. This maximizes the likelihood that her students will be able to successfully remember how to decode and remember the meaning of these words in the future.

In Ms. Peterson's lesson, we see evidence of moving instruction from being teacher-directed to student-directed. At the beginning of the lesson, the students are expected to try to independently complete their KWL charts. When her students protest that they do not know anything about the American Revolution, Ms. Peterson provides minimal prompting to reassure them they do already know a good deal. After the students complete each section of their charts, Mrs. Peterson has them share what they wrote, a way to check their mastery of the KWL technique and the subject matter while still encouraging independent completion of the task. Likewise, she has her students work independently to preview the features of the book they are reading. When she has her students share what they learned, she offers only minimal prompts to encourage the conversation and remind the students of the value of certain text features. She ends the lesson with a task for the students to complete independently (the exit card). By providing the students with repeated opportunities for independent execution of the KWL and previewing strategies, Mrs. Peterson scaffolds instruction so that it becomes increasingly student-directed.

CODA

These three teachers of intermediate level children reflected well the instructional tools promoted by Kameenui and Carnine (1998). We are only privileged with a snapshot of their skills so it is useful to think about other teaching regimens that may be incorporated in larger segments of instruction that would assist children with diverse learning needs. We would encourage the teachers to plan purposeful peer groups when dividing children for instruction. There is solid research evidence that pairing stronger and weaker readers in supplemental reading activities results in meaningful gains for both types of readers (Fuchs, Fuchs, and Burish 2000). Thus, we would recommend having a range of expertise within a group and to not exclusively group homogeneously. This strategy may have been useful to Ms. Gabriel in generating definitions and sentences with new vocabulary words. Teachers must be careful, however, to not assume that everyone understands just because one child had the correct answer. We also recommend that teachers monitor progress frequently and not just at the end of instructional units. By using formative assessments, teachers can analyze the effectiveness of their instruction and make changes when children are not progressing satisfactorily. By using such assessments to carefully monitor the progress of each child, teachers can modify their instruction to ensure that *all* students successfully master what is taught.

A Principal's Perspective

Kathy Lynn Brake

As the principal of one of the schools in this research study, I was asked to reflect upon what I felt makes the difference in developing a school community that exhibits and supports the kind of high-quality teaching seen in these lesson cases. Having been the principal of that school for fifteen years, I would be remiss if I did not describe our school. At the time of the study and ever since "adequate yearly progress" has been measured, our students have met the standards set by the state for each sub-group identified in No Child Left Behind (NCLB). Additionally, at the time of the study, the school had 55 percent of the student population receiving subsidized lunch and was also diverse, with the following demographic breakdown: 19.9 percent African American, 0.3 percent American Indian, 12.6 percent Asian, 44.9 percent Hispanic, 22.3 percent White, 13.1 percent special education, 33.1 percent ELL (English language learners). The children are served in a pre-kindergarten through fifth grade setting using the home-school model of special education full inclusion. The school also had a Head Start class for three-year-olds. So how does a school support high-quality teaching and what can a principal do to create and sustain that supportive climate?

PERSONAL RELATIONSHIP BUILDING AND HIGH EXPECTATIONS

Personal relationship building is important in order for children to feel supported during classroom instruction. The teacher cannot expect a child to feel confident in taking risks during the instructional period if that child does not feel safe in responding to questions posed. Children who feel that the environment in which they learn is free from criticism will often open and stretch their minds to new heights of learning. These same children need to be provided with scaffolding questions to lead them to successful responses. It is when this kind of climate has been established and emanates throughout the instructional day that children will have the confidence and encouragement to grow and learn.

Teachers are great enablers—they want and need for children to be successful, sometimes to the extent that they require different responses from different children. Teachers who are enablers often may not continue to challenge and stretch a child; they may ask lower-level questions and accept minimal responses, and when they do this they are not requiring the same learning from all children. Indeed, they are not using high-quality teaching skills. If we are going to narrow, no—if we are going to eliminate—the achievement gap, all staff must have high expectations for all children and must require all children to meet all instructional goals. In order to do this, some of our children will have to have instructional interventions provided to them that include scaffolding of instruction as well as previewing of skills to be learned, and that's what high-quality teachers do. They carefully monitor the learning of these children so that they can intervene appropriately in order for them to be successful on formative and summative assessments.

It is not only important for teachers to have personal relationships with students in their care, but it is equally important for administrators to exhibit these same skills with their staff. A stable, warm, inviting team-building climate must be a part of every school in order for staff and students to meet the high expectations required. You can often feel this kind of climate upon entering a building. You can most certainly feel it when it does not exist. Teachers who work in schools that exhibit a warm, inviting, collegial climate are more positive, have high energy, and become so inter-connected with each other and the community that they never want to leave. This kind of stable, caring staff works beyond what is required to collaborate and seek just the right strategy to meet the needs of each learner. Every child is owned by every staff member in the building. Every child's success is the direct result of this ownership.

According to Blankstein (2004), "The future of leadership must be embedded in the hearts and minds of the many, and not rest on the shoulders of a heroic few" (210). In order to sustain quality leadership in any school system, systems thinking must be applied to all initiatives. It is through this sense of teaming, where principals learn from other principals through support groups, that sustainability can occur. It is through this sense of teaming, where teachers learn from each other and become a support to each other, that sustainability can occur. In *The Fifth Discipline*, Peter Senge (1990) wrote, "Tackling a difficult problem is often a matter of seeing where the high leverage lies, a change which—with a minimum of effort—would lead to lasting significant improvement" (64). Perhaps the leverage point described by Senge is the professional learning community that is built within an individual school or within an individual grade level that focuses on discussing instructional implications after analyzing common formative assessments.

Peterson and Deal (2002) believe a school's culture has a powerful impact on what occurs daily in that school: "A school's culture sharpens the focus of daily behavior and increases attention to what is important and valued" (10). Whatever is valued in a school's culture will be done. If student achievement is an active ingredient of school culture, then staff will work collectively in that regard. It becomes the commitment by which the school lives. Productivity on the part of teachers and students increases when driven by positive school culture. If data collection, analysis, and interpretation are important to the members of a school community, they become a part of its culture. If teachers feel comfortable collaborating to determine needs for improvement in instruction and in reviewing data on a regular basis, then collaboration becomes a part of its culture. The culture of a school is and ought to be shaped by its leadership.

Principals and teachers must be willing to critically review the data, openly discuss the results found, and determine next steps in instruction. Teachers must learn to work closely together as a team to identify learning outcomes, determine what proficiency looks like, and then monitor the data they gather. They must learn to interact personally and daily with the data they gather. Principals must and should meet on a regular basis with school teams to discuss data and guide teachers in determining instructional implications. Principals must call upon specialists in their schools to help them guide these data discussions. A staff development teacher and reading specialist team working in concert with an administrator can be a valuable part of the grade-level data team discussions. The principal's presence is critical as teachers will increase their acceptance of the data through the supportive discussions about data. Conversations such as these will not be seen as a threat to their professional abilities, but as a support in helping the teachers increase student achievement. Every teacher upon entering the profession enters it because they want to help children learn and grow.

MONITORING

"The lifeblood of school improvement is student achievement data," (Rettig, McCullough, Santos, and Watson 2003, 73). Whether mandated by a federal law or imposed by taxpayers who require school systems to be more accountable, the regular and timely analysis of data should be an integral part of every instructional day. "Timely feedback provided throughout a learning experience is referred to as 'formative' assessment as opposed to 'summative' assessment that occurs at the end of a learning experience" (Marzano 2003, 37). Not only should principals and teachers analyze summative data to understand adequate yearly progress, they should also analyze formative data points in order to determine instructional implications and make adjustments to instruction in order to intervene early enough to improve the results of summative data.

School principals play an active role in analyzing and interpreting data in order to meet requirements made by their school systems and the federal government. Yet classroom teachers make the final determination as to what is actually taught on a daily basis. Therefore, it is critical for classroom teachers to increase their skills and abilities in data analysis and interpretation. Educational researchers have concluded that a teacher's use of formative assessments could improve the achievement of students (Marzano 2003).

Teachers, schools, states, the entire nation are struggling to close or eliminate the achievement gap for students. "While formative assessments can help all pupils, it yields particularly good results with low achievers by concentrating on specific problems of their work and giving them a clear understanding of what is wrong and how to put it right" (Black and Wiliam 1998, 6). Many teachers struggle to improve their instructional practices in an effort to achieve improved educational results with all of their children. If formative assessment is one way to close the achievement gap, then the careful, complete analysis and interpretation of formative assessment results should be an ongoing part of professional growth for every teacher.

In this age of accountability, good teaching will be determined by looking at results (Jerald 2003). Teachers need to look at the results of their students' formative assessments and be able to analyze them correctly in order to adapt their own instructional practices and make instructional changes related to their analysis. Rettig, McCullough, Santos, and Watson (2003) determined that teachers should work in teams to design and administer common assessments. It is through this collaborative effort that they analyze results and student progress becomes a school-wide concern (Rettig et al. 2003). We are fortunate to have a district-wide curriculum that includes such common assessments. It is imperative that staff is required to work collaboratively to analyze results and determine instructional implications.

Testing and assessment should be an integral part of the educational experience. If schools focus on the high-stakes testing required by the federal government instead of focusing on the instructional practices and formative assessments within the classrooms, they may only get short-term results. While the collecting of data is important to the educational process, it is the careful analysis and interpretation of that data that will change instruction: "While data analysis is the process of counting and comparing, interpreting is making sense of what the analysis tells us" (Killion 2003, 21). It is through this frequent analysis and interpretation of data that teachers will make the decisions that will benefit daily instruction. Therefore, focusing on teachers' instructional decision making after they have given formative assessments will ultimately have greater effects on student achievement and success.

STAFF DEVELOPMENT

Monitoring of data should help the school principal determine if individual classes or grade levels are meeting the school system's benchmarks, thus allowing specialized staff to intervene on an "as needed" basis to assist individual students or teachers. Formative assessment data are used while conferencing with and observing the progress of teachers. The focus of our school system is on internal, consistent staff development. All schools at every level (elementary, middle, and high) have full-time staff development teachers. All elementary schools have reading specialists. Many elementary schools have part-time math content coaches. These support specialists are a critical part of the achievement of students. It is through their conscious commitment to data review that they guide the staff development needs of the teachers in their school. Data are also used to support training needs after careful review from the reading specialist, math content coach, and staff development teacher. Principals may also use the results of these data to project success on state and system summative assessments. Also, administrators, grade-level teams, and support specialists may use these data to guide discussions about curriculum development and implementation, as well as determine the need for academic interventions for individual students. Knowledge of assessments and the ability to analyze and interpret them ought to be an important part of the principal's role as an instructional leader.

As teachers collaborate to identify strengths and weaknesses of instruction through data analysis, they may grow in their ability to refine instruction and teaching strategies to have greater impact on the academic achievement of students. Schmoker (2003) concluded that classroom teachers can learn to analyze data and, that by doing so, this analysis will have an impact on teaching and achievement. It is through careful analysis and interpretation of formative assessment data that instruction can change to allow students to achieve academic targets. Teams of teachers can learn to work together to analyze data relevant to them and the immediate instruction of their students. Often teachers are presented with summative data that make little sense to them in their daily decision making about instruction. These summative data are often presented at year's end or even at the beginning of the following year, when they cannot impact student instruction as needed in real time.

According to Schmoker (2003), "The primary purpose of analyzing data is improving instruction to achieve greater student success" (23). If analyzing data is critical to students' academic achievement, then those data should be formative data rather than summative, and teachers must be thoroughly trained in analyzing the data to inform instruction. Black and Wiliam (1998) concluded that assessments must be used to adjust teaching and learning in order for them to have a significant impact. The authors stated: "For assessment to function formatively, the results have to be used to adjust teaching and learning; thus a significant aspect of any program will be the ways in which teachers make these adjustments" (3).

PROFESSIONAL LEARNING COMMUNITIES

A professional learning community as defined by DuFour (2003) is one in which "the people have a clear sense of the mission they are to accomplish and a shared vision of the conditions they must create to achieve their mission" (15). He further believes that the entire school system must

> engage teams in a cycle of continuous improvement—gathering and analyzing data and information, identifying weaknesses and areas of concern, working together to develop strategies to address specific weaknesses and concerns, supporting each other as they implement those strategies, gathering new data and information to assess the impact of the strategies and then starting the process all over again. (15)

It is the expectation of our school system that schools and teacher teams will work as a professional learning community.

A strong effort was made in the school district to rewrite our reading and mathematics curriculums to focus on supporting special populations through the scaffolding of instruction to meet the needs of special education students and English language learners. But, in addition, the school system also has an expectation that all teachers will teach all children accelerated indicators. This new curriculum also connects system targets and instructional indicators to the recommended state curriculum. During common planning time teacher teams look closely at the indicators they are teaching to decide how they will monitor success and what multiple measures they will use to determine if a child has met proficiency and to discuss instructional implications and changes when their instruction has not been successful. It is taking on this responsibility for what a child learns that is also a sign of high-quality teaching.

Feedback to students is a critical part of this practice. "Teachers must possess and be ready to apply knowledge of sound classroom assessment practices" (Stiggins 2004, 26). The feedback a teacher gives on formative assessments is a critical part of a child's individual improvement. Black, Harrison, Lee, Marshall, and Wiliam (2004) stated that "feedback that focuses on what needs to be done can encourage all to believe that they can improve" (18). This kind of feedback enhances learning and supports the child to put forth the effort to achieve. By providing this kind of specific feedback educators are "building learning environments that help all students believe that they can succeed at hitting the target if they keep trying" (Stiggins 2004, 24).

In an effort to meet the ever-demanding accountability requirements thrust upon teachers, principals, and school systems by parents, the broader community, and the federal and state governments, one must focus on what occurs within the classroom setting as it directly impacts the instructional decisions being made by an individual classroom teacher. One must look at the use of formative assessments to guide instructional decision-making practices. Teachers need to look at assessment as a way to receive feedback about their students' learning so that they can adjust instruction and reteach concepts and skills students have not mastered. Working collaboratively in teacher teams and discussing common formative assessment results are important staff development practices. The degree of difference in a teacher's ability to analyze and interpret formative assessment data should make a difference in determining instructional implications and increasing student achievement.

PROFESSIONAL GROWTH SYSTEMS

Three professional growth systems have been developed and implemented by our school district: a teacher professional growth system, an administrator professional growth system, and a supporting services professional growth system. Leaders from all the employee representative organizations played an important role in shaping each professional growth system and each is important in supporting high-quality teaching. It was through much collaborative effort on the part of the executive staff of the school system that this was accomplished. It was an attempt on the part of the school system to improve development, training, retention, and evaluation of all staff.

As a part of the teacher and administrator professional growth systems, consulting teachers and consulting principals are assigned to novice employees and those not performing to standard. These consulting teachers and principals observe their clients and provide regular feedback to them on their practices. They are available to assist their clients in every way possible to ensure their professional success. They are also there to assist in confirming the practices of an underperforming client.

DATA, DATA, DATA

Educators know that the regular use of data analysis has its benefits in improving instruction. In fact, every competent, efficient organization agrees that data are imperative to the growth and success of any business or organization. Seldom does a day go by that data are not reviewed, analyzed, and interpreted for the benefit of the organization. In this age of accountability and with the large amounts of federal, state, and local monies being allocated for educational resources, the American public, elected officials, and local school systems demand an educational payback on their funding. In an effort to hold teachers and school systems accountable for the academic achievement of every child, data gathering and reporting are critical. Yearly summative assessments are only a small fraction of the accountability of student achievement. In order to meet the summative goal, school systems are moving to common formative assessments, monitoring and data gathering of learning indicators, and benchmarking academic growth in reading and mathematics on a regular basis as the school year progresses. To deal adequately with data:

- Teachers must learn to interact personally and daily with data they collect;
- Principals must meet on a regular basis with school teams to discuss data and guide teachers in determining instructional implications;
- Principals must call upon school specialists to help guide these data discussions; and
- During any staff development training, data discussions with teachers must always focus on instructional implications.

PARTNERSHIPS

Our school system has created several important part-nerships with universities in an effort to meet the career advancement needs of our support staff as well as increase the quality of teacher level candidates. One such part-nership was initially developed in an attempt to increase the number of minority and male teachers in the school system. Candidates with bachelor degrees are invited to apply to the Masters in Education program, and during this two-year, degree-seeking period, they are employed as paraeducators in the schools. As a school that has had many of these program interns for several years, I can attest to its success. From the first day on the job every intern in my school was encouraged to join the professional staff for all staff meetings and preservice trainings. They were plunged into the culture and climate of the school and af-ter the two-year program often remained at the school in teacher level positions. I was able to increase the number of male teachers and African American and Hispanic teach-ers through this program. Similar partnerships have been created with another university to increase the number of teacher candidates with special education degrees.

CONCLUSION

One might disagree with how individual states have inter-preted and implemented NCLB, but every educator knows that this federal law has caused each of us to look more closely at the performance of sub-groups. This has forced us to attack and—yes, with clear, high expectations—attempt to eliminate the achievement gap. Every educator with a conscience and a heart must certainly believe that no matter a child's ethnicity, no matter a child's poverty level, no matter the special needs or second language needs, every child must be encouraged and supported to perform at high academic levels. It is only when we do this that we will finally provide equal educational opportunity for all children.

References

Afflerbach, P., Pearson, P. D., and Paris, S. G. (2008). Clarifying differences between reading skills and reading strategies. *The Reading Teacher, 61*(5), 364–73.

Alexander, P. A., Graham, S., and Harris, K. (1998). A perspective on strategy research: Progress and prospects. [Special Issue]. *Educational Psychology Review, 10*, 129–54.

Alexander, P. A., and Murphy, P. K. (1998). The research base for APA's learner-centered psychological principles. In N. M. Lambert and B. L. McCombs (Eds.), *Issues in school reform: A sampler of psychological perspectives on learner-centered schools* (25–60). Washington, DC: The American Psychological Association.

Almasi, J. F. (2003). *Teaching strategic processes in reading.* New York: Guilford Press.

American Psychological Association Board of Educational Affairs. (1995, Dec.). Learner-centered psychological principles: A framework for school redesign and reform. Washington, DC: American Psychological Association. (www.apa.org/ed/lcp.html).

Anderson, R. C., and Pearson, P. D. (1984). A schema-theoretic view of basic processes in reading. In P. D. Pearson, R. Barr, M. L. Kamil, and P. Mosenthal (Eds.), *Handbook of reading research* (Vol. 1, 255–91). New York: Longman.

Barnett-Clarke, C. (2001). Case design and use: Opportunities and limitations. *Research in Science Education, 31*(2), 309–12.

Bear, D. R., and Templeton, S. (1998). Explorations in developmental spelling: Foundations for learning and teaching phonics, spelling, and vocabulary. *The Reading Teacher, 52,* 222–42.

Blachowicz, C. L. Z., and Fisher, P. (2000). Vocabulary instruction. In M. L. Kamil, P. B. Mosenthal, P. D. Pearson, and R. Barr (Eds.), *Handbook of reading research* (Vol. 3, 255–91). Mahwah, NJ: Erlbaum.

Black, P., Harrison, C., Lee, C., Marshall, B., and Wiliam, D. (2004). Working inside the black box: Assessment for learning in the classroom. *Phi Delta Kappan, 86*(1), 9–21.

Black, P., and Wiliam, D. (1998). Inside the black box: Raising standards through classroom assessment. *Phi Delta Kappan, 80*(2), 139–48.

Blankstein, A. M. (2004). *Failure is not an option.* Thousand Oaks, CA: Corwin Press.

Bransford, J. D., Brown, A. L., and Cocking, R. R. (Eds.). (1999). *How people learn: Brain, mind, experience, and school.* Washington, DC: National Academy of Science.

Brinckloe, J. (1985/1986). *Fireflies!* New York: Macmillan and Aladdin.

Brown, R., Pressley, M., Van Meter, P., and Schuder, T. (1996). A quasi-experimental validation of transactional strategies instruction with low-achieving second-grade readers. *Journal of Educational Psychology, 88,* 18–37.

Carruth, E. K. (1966). *She wanted to read: The story of Mary McLeod Bethune.* Nashville, TN: Abingdon Press.

Carter, K. (1999). What is a case? What is not a case? In M. A. Lundeberg, B. Levin, and H. Harrington (Eds.), *Who learns what from cases and how? The research base for teaching and learning with cases* (165–75). Mahwah, NJ: Lawrence Erlbaum.

Cazden, C. B. (1988). *Classroom discourse: The language of teaching and learning.* Portsmouth, NH: Heinemann.

Chall, J. (1983). *Learning to read: The great debate.* New York: McGraw-Hill.

Chambliss, M., and Graeber, A. (2003, April). Does subject matter *matter?* Paper presented at the meeting of the American Educational Research Association, Chicago.

Clare, L., and Gallimore, R. (1996). Using moral dilemmas in children's literature as a vehicle for moral education and teaching reading comprehension. *Journal of Moral Education, 25*(3), 325–42.

Clark, K. F., and Graves, M. F. (2004). Scaffolding students' comprehension of text. *The Reading Teacher, 58,* 570–80.

Common Core State Standards Initiative. Retrieved December 5, 2010, from www.corestandards.org/.

Cousins, M. (1952). *Ben Franklin of old Philadelphia.* New York: Random House.

Coyne, M. D., Kameenui, E. J., and Simmons, D. C. (2001). Prevention and intervention in beginning reading: Two complex systems. *Learning Disabilities Research and Practice, 16,* 62–73.

Daniels, H. (2002). *Literature circles: Voice and choice in the student-centered classroom.* Portland, ME: Stenhouse.

Doctorow, M., Wittrock, M. C., and Marks, C. (1978). Generative processes in reading comprehension. *Journal of Educational Psychology, 70,* 109–18.

Duffy, G. G., Roehler, L. R., Sivan, E., Rackliffe, G., Book, C., Meloth, M., et al. (1987). Effects of explaining the reasoning associated with using reading strategies. *Reading Research Quarterly. 22,* 347–68.

DuFour, R. (2003). Building a professional learning community. *The School Administrator, 60*(5), 13–18.

Fenstermacher, G. D. (2001). On the concept of manner and its visibility in teaching practice. *Journal of Curriculum Studies, 33*(6), 639–53.

Fenstermacher, G. D., Osguthorpe, R. D., and Sanger, M. N. (2009). Teaching morally and teaching morality. *Teacher Education Quarterly, 36*(3), 7–19.

Fisher, P. J. L., Blachowicz, C. L. Z., and Smith, J. C. (1991). Vocabulary learning in literature discussion groups. In J. Zutell and S. McCormick (Eds.), Learner factors/teacher factors: Issues in literacy research and instruction (pp. 201–9). *Fortieth yearbook of the National Reading Conference.* Chicago: National Reading Conference.

Fleischman, P. (1991). *The borning room.* New York: HarperCollins.

Fritz, J. (1987). *The cabin faced west.* New York: Penguin Group.

Fuchs, D., Fuchs, L. S., and Burish, P. (2000). Peer-assisted learning strategies: An evidence-based practice to promote reading achievement. *Learning Disabilities Research and Practice, 15,* 85–91.

Gambrell, L. B., and Bales, R. J. (1986). Mental imagery and the comprehension-monitoring performance of fourth- and fifth-grade readers. *Reading Research Quarterly, 21*, 454–64.

Gersten, R., Fuchs, L. S., Williams, J. P., and Baker, S. (2001). Teaching reading comprehension strategies to students with learning disabilities: A review of research. *Review of Educational Research, 71*, 279–320.

Goldman, S. R., and Rakestraw, J. A. (2000). Structural aspects of constructing meaning from text. In M. L. Kamil, P. B. Mosenthal, P. D. Pearson, and R. Barr (Eds.), *Handbook of reading research* (Vol. 3, 311–35). Mahwah, NJ: Lawrence Erlbaum Associates.

Grossman, P. (2005). Research on pedagogical approaches in teacher education. In M. Cochran-Smith and K. M. Zeichner (Eds.), *Studying teacher education: A report of the AERA panel on research and teacher education* (425–76). Mahway, NJ: Lawrence Erlbaum.

Grossman, P., Schoenfeld, A., and Lee, C. (2005). Teaching subject matter. In L. Darling-Hammond and J. Bransford (Eds.), *Preparing teachers for a changing world: What teachers should learn and be able to do* (201–31). San Francisco: Jossey-Bass.

Guthrie, J. T., and Wigfield, A. (2000). Engagement and motivation in reading. In M. L. Kamil, P. B. Mosenthal, P. D. Pearson, and R. Barr (Eds.), *Handbook of reading research* (Vol. 3, 403–22). Mahwah, NJ: Erlbaum.

Hansen, D. T. (2001). Teaching as a moral activity. In V. Richardson (Ed.), *Handbook of research on teaching* (826–57). Washington, DC: American Educational Research Association.

Hudson, R. F., Lane, H. B., and Pullen, P. C. (2005). Reading fluency assessment and instruction: What, why, and how? *The Reading Teacher, 58*, 702–14.

International Reading Association and National Council of Teachers of English (IRA and NCTE). (1996). *Standards for the English language arts.* Newark, DE: International Reading Association.

Jackson, P. W. (1986). *The practice of teaching.* New York: Teachers College Press.

Jerald, C. (2003). Beyond the rock and the hard place. *Educational Leadership, 61*(3), 12–16.

Kameenui, E. J., and Carnine, D. W. (1998). *Effective teaching strategies that accommodate diverse learners.* Upper Saddle River, NJ: Merrill.

Kamil, M., Mosenthal, P., Pearson, P. D., and Barr, R. (Eds.). (2000). *Handbook of reading research, Volume III*. Mahwah, NJ: Lawrence Erlbaum.

Killion, J. (2003). 8 smooth steps. *The Journal of the National Staff Development Council, 24*(4), 14–21.

Kilpatrick, J., Swafford, J., and Findell, B. (Eds.). (2001). *Adding it up: Helping children learn mathematics*. Washington, DC: National Academy Press and the National Reading Council, Mathematics Learning Study Committee, Center for Education, Division of Behavioral and Social Sciences and Education.

Kuhn, M. R. (2005). A comparative study of small group fluency instruction. *Reading Psychology, 26*, 127–46.

Kuhn, M. R., and Stahl, S. (2003). Fluency: A review of developmental and remedial strategies. *The Journal of Educational Psychology, 95*, 1–19.

Leach, J. M., Scarborough, H. S., and Rescorla, L. (2003). Late-emerging reading disabilities. *Journal of Educational Psychology, 95*, 211–24.

Learner-Centered Principles Work Group of the APA Board of Educational Affairs (1997, November). *Learner-centered psychological principles: a framework for school reform and redesign*. Washington, DC: American Psychological Association.

Levin, B. (1999). The role of discussion in case pedagogy: Who learns what? And how? In M. A. Lundeberg, B. Levin, and H. Harrington (Eds.), *Who learns what from cases and how? The research base for teaching and learning with cases* (139–57). Mahwah, NJ: Lawrence Erlbaum.

Lundeberg, M. A., and Scheurman, G. (1997). Looking twice means seeing more: Developing pedagogical knowledge through case analysis. *Teaching and Teacher Education, 13*(8), 783–97.

Lunn, J. (1985). *The root cellar*. New York: The Penguin Group.

Marzano, R. J. (2003). *What works in schools: Translating research into action*. Alexandria, VA: Association for Supervision and Curriculum Development.

Merseth, K. (1996). Cases and case methods in teacher education. In J. Sikula, T. Buttery, and E. Guyton (Eds.), *Handbook of research on teacher education* (2nd edition, 722–44). New York: MacMillan.

Mitchell, M. (1993). Situational interest. Its multifaceted structure in the secondary school mathematics classroom. *Journal of Educational Psychology, 85*, 424–36.

Moore, K. (1998). *If you lived at the time of the American Revolution*. New York: Scholastic.

Morrow, L. M., Wamsley, G., Duhammel, K., and Fittipaldi, N. (2002). A case study of exemplary practice in fourth grade. In B. M. Taylor and P. D. Pearson (Eds.), *Teaching reading: Effective schools, accomplished teachers* (289–307). Mahwah, NJ: Lawrence Erlbaum Associates, Publishers.

Murakami, H. (1997). *The wind-up bird chronicle*. New York: Random House.

National Reading Panel (NRP). (2000). *Teaching children to read: An evidenced-based assessment of the scientific research literature on reading and its implications for reading instruction: Reports of the subgroups*. Bethesda, MD: National Institute of Child Health and Human Development.

Noddings, N. (1984). *Caring: A feminine approach to ethics and moral education*. Berkeley: University of California Press.

Ogle, D.M. (1986). K-W-L: A teaching model that develops active reading of expository text. *Reading Teacher, 39,* 564–70.

Oxford, R. (Ed.). (1996). *Language learning strategies around the world: Crosscultural perspectives*. Manoa: University of Hawaii Press.

Oxford, R. L., Cho, Y., Leung, S., and Kim, H-J. (2004). Effect of the presence and difficulty of a task on reading strategy use: An exploratory study. *International Review of Applied Linguistics and Language Teaching, 42*(1), 1–42.

Paris, S., Cross, D., and Lipson, M. (1984). Informed strategies for learning: A program to improve children's reading awareness and comprehension. *Journal of Educational Psychology, 76,* 1239–52.

Paris, S. G., Lipson, M. Y., and Wixson, K. K. (1983). Becoming a strategic reader. *Contemporary Educational Psychology, 8,* 293–316.

Peterson, K. D., and Deal, T. E. (2002). *The shaping school culture fieldbook*. San Francisco: Jossey-Bass.

Pressley, G. M. (1976). Mental imagery helps eight-year-olds remember what they read. *Journal of Educational Psychology, 68,* 355–59.

Pressley, M. and Afflerbach, P. (1995). *Verbal protocols of reading: The nature of constructively responsive reading*. Hillsdale, NJ: Erlbaum.

Pressley, M., and Wharton-McDonald, R. (2006). The need for increased comprehension instruction. In M. Pressley (Ed.) *Reading instruction that works: The case for balanced instruction* (3rd edition, 293–346).

New York: Guilford Press.

Pressley, M., El-Dinary, P. B., Gaskins, I., Schuder, T., Bergman, J. L., Almas, J., and Brown, R. (1992). Beyond direct explanation: Transactional instruction of reading comprehension strategies. *The Elementary School Journal, 95*, 513–55.

Rettig, M. D., McCullough, L. L., Santos, K., and Watson, C. (2003). A blueprint for increasing student achievement. *Educational Leadership, 61*(3), 71–76.

Rice, L. (1995, Nov.). Pandas in peril. *Boy's Life, 85*(11), 20–23.

Richards, M. (2000). Be a good detective: Solve the case of oral reading fluency. *The Reading Teacher, 53*, 534–39.

Schmoker, M. (2003). First things first: Demystifying data analysis. *Educational Leadership, 60*(5), 22–24.

Schwartz, R. M., and Raphael, T. E. (1985). Concept of definition: A key to improving students' vocabulary. *The Reading Teacher, 39*, 198–205.

Senge, P. M. (1990). *The fifth discipline: The art and practice of the learning organization.* New York: Doubleday.

Shulman, J. (1992). Introduction. In J. Shulman (Ed.), *Case methods in teacher education* (xiii–xvii). New York: Teachers College Press.

Shulman, L. (1987). Knowledge and teaching: Foundations of the new reform. *Harvard Educational Review, 57*(1), 1–22.

———. (1992). Toward a pedagogy of cases. In J. Shulman (Ed.), *Case methods in teacher education* (1–33). New York: Teachers College Press.

———. (2004). Just in case: reflections on learning from experience. In S. Wilson (Ed.), *The wisdom of practice: Essays on teaching, learning, and learning to teach* (463–82). San Francisco: Jossey-Bass.

Silverstein, S. (1974). *Where the sidewalk ends.* New York: HarperCollins.

Starratt, R. J. (2005). Cultivating the moral character of learning and teaching: A neglected dimension of educational leadership. *School Leadership and Management, 25*(4), 399–411.

Stein, N. L., and Glenn, C. F. (1979). An analysis of story comprehension in elementary school children. In R. O. Freedle (Ed.), *New directions in discourse processing: Vol. 2, Advances in discourse processes* (53–120). Norwood, NJ: Ablex.

Stevens, R., Wineburg, S., Herrenkohl, L. R., and Bell, P. (2005). Comparative understanding of school subjects: Past, present, and future. *Review of Educational Research, 75*(2), 125–57.

Stiggins, R. (2004). New assessment beliefs for a new school mission. *Phi Delta Kappan*, *86*(1), 22–27.

Taylor, B. M., and Pearson, P. D. (Eds.). (2002). *Teaching reading: Effective schools, accomplished teachers.* Mahwah, NJ: Erlbaum

Templeton, S., and Morris, D. (2000). Spelling. In M. L. Kamil, P. B. Mosenthal, P. D. Pearson, and R. Barr (Eds.), *Handbook of reading research* (Vol. 3, 525–43). Mahwah, NJ: Lawrence Erlbaum Associates.

Tom, A. R. (1984). *Teaching as a moral craft.* New York: Longman.

Valli. L. (1990). Moral approaches to reflective practice. In R. T. Clift, W. R. Houston, and M. C. Pugach (Eds.), *Encouraging reflective practice in education: An analysis of issues and programs* (57–72). New York: Teachers College Press.

Valli, L., and Croninger, R. (2001). *High-quality teaching of foundational skills in mathematics and reading.* Washington, DC: National Science Foundation Interdisciplinary Educational Research Initiative.

Valli, L., Croninger, R., Alexander, P., Chambliss, M., Graeber, A., and Price, J. (2004, April). A study of high-quality teaching: Mathematics and reading. Symposium paper presented at the annual meeting of the American Educational Research Association. San Diego, CA.

Walsh, J. P. (1982). *The green book.* New York: Farrar, Straus, and Giroux.

Walter, M. P. (1986). *Justin and the best biscuits in the world.* New York: Random House.

Wilkinson, L. C., and Silliman, E. R. (2000). Classroom language and literacy learning. In M. L. Kamil, P. B. Mosenthal, P. D. Pearson, and R. Barr (Eds.), *Handbook of reading research* (Vol. 3, 337–60). Mahwah, NJ: Lawrence Erlbaum Associates.

Williams, J. (2003). Teaching text structure to improve reading. In K. R. Harris, H. L. Swanson, and S. Graham (Eds.), *Handbook of learning disabilities* (30–56). New York: Guilford.

Wilson, S. (1992). A case concerning content: Using case studies to teach about subject matter. In J. Shulman (Ed.), *Case methods in teacher education* (64–89). New York: Teachers College Press.

Worthy, J., and Broaddus, K. (2002). Fluency beyond the primary grades: From performance to silent, independent reading. *The Reading Teacher, 55*, 334–43.

Yep. L. (1996). *The lost garden.* New York: Simon and Schuster.

Index

About the Contributors

THE AUTHORS

Marilyn Chambliss is associate professor emerita in the Department of Curriculum and Instruction. An educational psychologist, with a Ph.D. from Stanford, she is interested in how reading instruction and written materials can be designed to enhance the reading comprehension of all children. Her work has included describing comprehension processes that fourth/fifth graders use when they read different types of text and exploring how they could be taught to read more critically. She also has developed a system for analyzing the comprehensibility and learnability of social studies, science, and language arts textbooks, which she has taught to several hundred preservice teachers, practicing teachers, and district administrators.

Linda Valli is the inaugural Jeffrey and David Mullan Professor of Teacher Education and Professional Development in the Department of Curriculum and Instruction at the University of Maryland. She has a Ph.D. from the Department of Education Policy Studies at the University of Wisconsin, Madison and served for ten years as the director of teacher education at the Catholic University of America, where she developed a research-based teacher education program and used cases in her own teaching. She now teaches graduate courses on research on teaching, professional development, and action research. Her publications focus on the context of teaching, learning to teach, culturally responsive pedagogy, and education policy. She has extensive experience in ethnographic and qualitative research methodology.

COMMENTATORS

Patricia Alexander is a distinguished scholar-teacher and professor in the Department of Human Development at the University of Maryland with research interests in the areas of expertise, domain learning, reading, and strategic processing.

Kathy Lynn Brake is a regional administrator who oversees school performance in a large public school district. Formerly an elementary school principal for fifteen years, she has her doctorate in educational leadership from Bowie State University.

Daria Buese is an assistant professor at McDaniel College with interests in teaching expertise, teacher roles, and the moral dimensions of teaching.

Rose Marie Codling is a senior lecturer in the Reading Center at the Department of Curriculum and Instruction at the University of Maryland who specializes in reading assessment and diagnosis.

Sara J. Hines is an assistant professor in the Department of Special Education at Hunter College whose research interests include interventions for children with severe reading disabilities.

Rebecca Oxford is a distinguished scholar-teacher and professor emerita of second language education in the Department of Curriculum and Instruction at the University of Maryland with interests in motivation, strategies, socially mediated learning, and technology. Her current appointment is at the Air University where she is professor of language education and research in the Language Department of the U.S. Air Force Culture and Language Center.

Christine Peterson-Tardif has been a fourth to sixth grade teacher in a large public school system for eight years. She has a bachelor's degree in animal science and a master's degree in education, both from the University of Maryland.

Heather Ruetschlin Schugar specialized in reading education as a doctoral student at the University of Maryland and is now an assistant professor in the Department of Literacy at West Chester University of Pennsylvania. Her current lines of inquiry include research with informational text comprehension and e-Text comprehension. Additionally, she is actively involved with the Philadelphia Writing Project. She participated in the High-Quality Teaching study, piloted the cases in her undergraduate reading methods class, and wrote commentaries for the Facilitator's Guide.

Deborah L. Speece is a professor in the Department of Special Education at the University of Maryland who specializes in the area of reading development and learning disabilities.

Caroline Y. Walker is a doctoral candidate in the Department of Special Education at the University of Maryland whose interests include later developing reading disabilities, their classification, and remediation.